COLLECTOR'S ENCYCLOPEDIA OF

Cookie JARS

BOOK III

Fred Roerig
and
Joyce Herndon Roerig

COLLECTOR BOOKS
A Division of Schroeder Publishing Co., Inc.

The current values in this book should be used only as a guide. They are not intended to set prices, which vary from one section of the country to another. Auction prices as well as dealer prices vary greatly and are affected by condition as well as demand. Neither the Authors nor the Publisher assumes responsibility for any losses that might be incurred as a result of consulting this guide.

Searching For A Publisher?

We are always looking for knowledgeable people considered to be experts within their fields. If you feel that there is a real need for a book on your collectible subject and have a large comprehensive collection, contact Collector Books.

ON THE COVER:
Happy Memories limited edition Elvis Presley cookie jar, $300.00.
McCoy Engine with Smoke cookie jar prototype, price not determined.
Cookie Jarrin' Smokey Bear Bust cookie jar, $89.95.
Metlox Hobby Horse, $600.00 – 650.00.
Cookie Jarrin' Smokey Bear 2-piece salt and pepper set, $39.95.
Cookie Jarrin' Smokey Bear full-bodied bank, $49.95.
Sigma the Tastesetter Yoda bank, $60.00 – 70.00.
Sigma the Tastesetter Yoda salt and pepper set, $200.00+.
DeForest Lil Angel, $725.00 – 775.00.
Cookie Jarrin' Smokey Bear head bank, $29.95.

Cover design by Beth Summers
Book design by Beth Ray

Additional copies of this book may be ordered from:

COLLECTOR BOOKS
P.O. Box 3009
Paducah, Kentucky 42002-3009
or
Fred & Joyce Roerig
Route 2, Box 504
Walterboro, SC 29488

@$24.95. Add $2.00 for postage and handling.

ACKNOWLEDGMENTS

As it takes a village to raise a child, it takes the cookie jar community to responsibly "construct" a price guide. Without the corroboration of the following collectors, dealers, and collectors/dealers across the country, this newest volume of the *Collector's Encyclopedia of Cookie Jars* would not have been possible. These individuals unselfishly contributed photographs, well researched copy, and realistic cross-country pricing. A special thank you to the following: Debbie Dykstra, Campe Verde, AZ; Harvey Takasugi, Los Angeles, CA; Linda Romberg, Scottsdale, AZ; Bill and Loretta Hamburg, Woodland Hills, CA; Bonnie Beckerson, Hermosa Beach, CA; Diana Andrews, San Clemente, CA; Jack and Margaret DeForest, CA; Mike and Barbara Schwarz d.b.a. Past and Presents, Vacaville, CA; Joan Howard, Napa, CA; John Martin, Huntington Beach, CA; Keith and Judy Lytle d.b.a. Cookie Jar Antiques, Antioch, CA; Mary Potter, Cerritos, CA; Patsy Mello, Tulare, CA; Rich and Linda Guffey, El Cajon, CA; Richard Ochoa, Pleasanton, CA; Dallas and Wilma Reed, Denver CO; Glenn and Sherry Firestone, Miami, FL; Peter Gemmi, W. Palm Beach, FL; Carlie and Bennie Nell Coley, Alma, GA; Gail Levites, Savannah, GA; Dennis and Betty Oltmanns, Anamosa, IA; Joe Divine, Council Bluffs, IA; Loretta DeLozier, Bedford, IA; Russ and Linda Dial, Blackfoot, ID; Albert Speenburgh, Plano, IL; Jay Blumenfeld, Chicago, IL; Lee Gorman, Springfield, IL; Lorie Wuttke, St. Charles, IL; Mercedes and Hillary DiRenzo, Chicago, IL; Charlie's Collectibles, Independence, KS; Sandy Ernst, LaCygne, KS; Louise Maxwell, Lafayette, LA; Cam Curtis, Bel Air, MD; Jerry and Lona Spier, Reading, MI; Kathy Wolfe, W. Bloomfield, MI; Lyn Boone, Ypsilanti, MI; Michele Bady, Romulus, MI; Mike and Sue Davis, Ypsilanti, MI; Katherine Combs, Baltimore, MD; Antiques Mercantile, Marshfield, MO; Helen Smart, Republic, MO; Juarine Wooldridge, Mt. Vernon MO; Steve Niccum, MO; Nailah Azzam, Rosemount, MN; Chiquita Prestwood, Lenoir, NC; George Williams, Cary, NC; Raymond Davis, Asheville, NC; Jan and Mylo Candee, Bismarck, ND; Barbara and Arnie Gerr Brigantine, NJ; Joanne Lindberg, Metuchen, NJ; Ralph Porto, Montville, NJ; Michael and Shelley Buonaiuto, Santa Fe, NM; Diana Darrow, DeRuyter, NY; George and Barbara Honchar, Greenwood Lake, NY; Glenn Appleman, Booklyn, NY; Harvey Duke, Brooklyn, NY; Kathleen Moloney, Greenwood Lake, NY; Mark McMahon, New York, NY; Darlene Parsons d.b.a. Tally Ho Studio, Canton, OH; Paul Hoadley, Nashport, OH; Cecil Rapp, Columbus, OH; Dan Eggert and Carol Seman, Brecksville, OH; Gary and Mimi Rhinehimer, Cincinnati, OH; Tony Burns, Indianapolis, IN; Barbara Crews, Bethany, OK; Jack and Carol Jessen, Pittsburgh, PA; Jim and Carol Boshears, Pittsburgh, PA; Judy Posner, Effort, PA; Sylvia Tompkins, Lancaster, PA; Bill Roerig, Walterboro, SC; Herndon Joseph Roerig, Walterboro, SC; Jane Johnson, Walterboro, SC; John and Kay Grooms, Cayce, SC; Joy Roerig, Walterboro, SC; Lloyd and Doris Slyce, Lexington, SC; Paula Herndon Polk, Walterboro, SC; Diane Cauwels, Murfreesboro, TN; Ellen Reed, Friendship, TN; Betsey Edmondson, Plano, TX; Charles Mouton, Garland, TX; Deborah Robertson, Rockwall, TX; Helen Banuelos, Houston, TX; Gale Sachitano, Sourlake, TX; John Grogan, Mesquite, TX; Juanita Phelps, Tolar, TX; Loretta Anderson, Rockwall, TX; Paul and Debbie Zimmerman, Henderson, TX; Shari Armstrong, San Antonio, TX; Steve and Joyce Horelica, Angleton, TX; Tanya McNab, Fair Oaks Ranch, TX; Tommy Chapman, O'Brien TX; Richard Robar, Salt Lake City, UT; Roy and Nancy Demory, Nokesville, VA; Jerry and Kathy Whetstine, Stanwood, WA; Herb and Donna Timmerman, West Bend, WI; Jerry Oscarson, Janesville, WI; Karen Wuttke, Delavan, WI; and Tom Fralish, Berlin, WI. If we have inadvertently omitted anyone, we apologize, and say, thank you!

DEDICATION

INTRODUCTION

Browsing through the introductions in *Books I* and *II,* I reminisce. *Book I* spoke of happy times, adventures, a family intertwined with collecting cookie jars. Times changed; *Book II* mentions rising prices and reproductions.

Where are we today? Prices are stabilizing; reproductions are still around, creating uncertainty among new collectors and inexperienced dealers. Our newest feature on reproductions helps address this issue. It is a start.

A broad range of new cookie jars is flooding the market place. Manufacturers have expanded their lines with exciting new designs to attract the collector market; some of these are limited editions and artist-designed jars. All this activity has been stimulated by the high prices commanded by desirable cookie jars.

These are challenging times for cookie jar collectors; the more you know, the better prepared you are to deal with the challenges.

HINTS TO COLLECTORS

Buy what you like.

Consider you options. There are many ways to collect. You can gather a little bit (or a whole lot) of just about everything, collect in categories such as head jars, fruits and/or vegetables, maybe space related, or select a theme such as advertising, Black Americana, characters, Walt Disney, Warner Brothers, or restrict yourself to one specific pottery company.

Some collectors, who consider themselves purists, collect only old cookie jars. The older cookie jars are a limited commodity; there will be no more.

Age is not the only determinant of value. And just because a jar is old does not necessarily make it collectible.

Enhance your collection. Searching for matching go-withs such as salt and pepper shakers, banks, figurines, and non-ceramic items such as telephones, books, and dolls that relate to the jar keeps collecting interesting and fun, and enhances the display.

Remember, what you see in print isn't necessarily so. Not every author practices responsible journalism. Know your source.

If you are a new collector longing for those wonderful old(er) jars, it is probably wise to buy them now if they are within your budget. We feel they are not going to get cheaper. This does not mean jump at the first offer. Shop around. Compare prices. Buy from dealers you are comfortable with. It's a small world; it doesn't take many inquiries to accurately ascertain the reputation of a dealer. Just make certain you are not checking with a disgruntled or jealous rival.

Beware of scalpers! Most dealers offer new cookie jars at fair retail prices, choosing to exclude new jars from Warner Brothers, Viacom, and those exclusive to the Disney theme parks, stores, and catalog. They cannot (and should not) compete. Check out your local Disney and Warner Brothers stores and the 800 directory for listings of major companies. The Internet is another good source for information. Many companies have web sites. Should you choose not to buy when something is readily available, do not complain about prices on the secondary market after an item is discontinued.

Think twice about buying reproductions and/or unlicensed character cookie jars — then walk away.

As well as unlicensed reproductions, there are new unlicensed cookie jars. One (now) entitled Blowin' Smoke bears a remarkable resemblance to the advertising icon Joe Camel. There's a Dr. Suess Cat in the Hat (with matching salt and pepper shakers) and even a UPS Delivery truck to tantalize us. Persuasive marketing can lead us in the wrong direction. Make certain the individual with whom you are dealing is not saying "gotcha" all the way to the bank. Apply the rule above.

However, we have long felt licensed, limited edition cookie jars will become collectible in varying degrees. Time and supply and demand are the determining factors.

Most commemoratives are nothing more than glorified reproductions. They will never attain the value of the original.

Looking for adventure? Attend the National Cookie Jar Show held yearly, the first weekend in May, at the State Fairgrounds in Nashville, Tennessee. Even experienced collectors are in awe at the sight of all those fabulous cookie jars and matching go-withs in one room. We never fail to learn each and every trip. Y'all come!

A LITTLE COMPANY

A Little Company, located at 131 Sam Street, Santa Fe, New Mexico, was introduced in *Collector's Encyclopedia of Cookie Jars, Book II* with the company's history and works to date (1994).

Row 1: *Dolphin Boy*, 11" high, limited edition of 300. "A Little CO ©1994."
The boy can be either white or black; goes nicely with Delfina.   Issue price, $180.00

Delfina, 7½" high, limited edition of 300. "A Little CO ©1994." Choice
of skin and dress color; gold starfish and silver stars on dress.   Issue price, $180.00

Row 2: *Delfina*, 7½" high, limited edition of 300. "A Little CO ©1994." Choice
of skin and dress color; gold starfish and silver stars on dress.   Issue price, $180.00

Dolphin Boy, 11" high, limited edition of 300. "A Little CO ©1994." The
boy can be either white or black; goes nicely with Delfina.   Issue price, $180.00

Below: *Santa Fe Railroad Station*, 8" high. "A Little CO ©1993." The present
Santa Fe Railroad Station at the Guadalupe Street rail yards was built in
1908 of stuccoed brick in the California Mission style. This structure
complete with tile roof, replaced a simple four-room wooden building
(circa 1880). The 18-mile rail spur from Lamy to Santa Fe was
built in the late 1800s and connected the then isolated town of Santa Fe
to the main continental rail system. This cookie jar, a stylized version
of the station, is the only non-figurative jar to date from A Little Company.
Care has been taken to preserve this beautiful building's line and color.
On the back are graceful arches and more windows, and the loading
platform is complete with waiting luggage.   Issue price, $160.00

Josephine Baker, 11" high, limited edition of 650. "ALC" recessed
into the bottom of the jar. Also marked, "A Little CO ©1996." A beautiful
woman of extraordinary spirit and presence, a gifted performer who
knew how to exalt her animal nature as part of her human persona, makes
a stunning presentation. Mother-of-pearl luster is applied to the
pearls and, while the color may vary, the plumes are
primarily teal or pink.   Issue price, $225.00

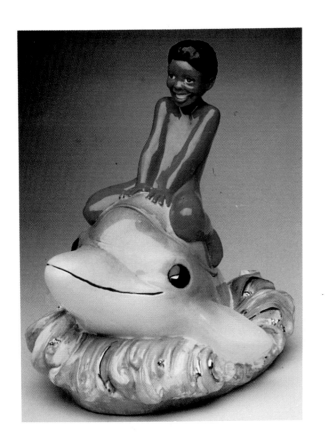

Row 1: *Bella (Dancer)*, 12", "ALC" incised into bottom of base. Limited edition of 500 with gold and silver trim. Captures the love of the dance, "A Little CO ©1995." Issue price, $150.00

Amosi (Drummer), 14½", limited edition of 500 with gold and silver trim. "A Little CO 1995." All over the United States people are learning the beautiful, sensual, and energetic dances of Haiti and the intricate, entrancing rhythms of the drums that power them. The style is a continuation of previous work, but more delicate and sculptural, with deep attention to the rhythm the drummer is creating. Issue price, $150.00

Row 2: *Carmella,* 13½" high, limited edition of 750. "ALC" incised into clay on bottom. "A Little Company, ©" and date (1997) written in underglaze. Issue price, $180.00

Ruby, 13", limited edition of 500. "A Little CO 1995 ©." Ruby's dress is deep satin blue (with gold and silver trim), reminiscent of the '40s. Her mood and posture suggest the rich velvet voice of that period. Issue price, $180.00

Below: *Secret Girls,* 12" high, limited edition of 750. "ALC" incised into clay on bottom. "A Little Company, ©" and date (1997) written in underglaze. Issue price, $190.00

Duet, 14" high, limited edition of 750. "ALC" incised into clay on bottom. "A Little Company, ©" and date (1997) written in underglaze. Issue price, $190.00

ABINGDON

with
"The clear ring of fine china."

Abingdon Pottery Company of Abingdon, Illinois, produced their first cookie jar in 1939. Twenty-three examples with color and design variations are featured in *The Collector's Encyclopedia of Cookie Jars Book I.*

A decorated Hippo and Hippo Bar Jar are featured in *Book II* with the Pumpkin and rare 21"-high Aunt Jemima.

Though Abingdon did not offer a large variety of cookie jar shapes, dedicated Abingdon collectors, like Shawnee collectors, seek color and design variations. Kathleen Moloney displays her Abingdon ladies to their best advantage, an excellent example of what cookie jars should be, a truly fun collectible.

Row 1:	*Little Old Lady,* "471."	$375.00 – 425.00
	Little Old Lady, "Abingdon USA 471."	$575.00 – 625.00
	Little Old Lady, "Abingdon USA 471."	$175.00 – 200.00
Row 2:	*Little Old Lady,* "Abingdon USA 471."	$175.00 – 200.00
	Little Old Lady, "Abingdon USA 471."	$175.00 – 200.00
	Little Old Lady, "Abingdon USA 471." Dec. "B."	$300.00 – 325.00
	Little Old Lady, "Abingdon USA 471."	$175.00 – 200.00
Row 3:	*Little Old Lady,* "Abingdon USA 471." Dec. "A"	$300.00 – 325.00
	Little Old Lady, "Abingdon USA 471." Dec. "C"	$575.00 – 625.00
	Little Old Lady, "Abingdon USA 471." Dec. "B"	$300.00 – 325.00
	Little Old Lady, "Abingdon USA 471." Dec. "A"	$300.00 – 325.00
Below:	*Abingdon Special,* produced for one year (1942). The top has "471" incised; the base, "561" and "Abingdon USA" stamp. Extremely rare. Moloney.	$500.00 – 600.00

ADVERTISING

The collecting of advertising cookie jars continues to gain in popularity. Many companies, like Nabisco, offer a wide assortment. For example, in Nabisco's 1995 Holiday Catalog only one cookie jar was offered, the *Chips Ahoy* cylinder. There were numerous tins, promotional clothing and decorator items, but just one cookie jar. The 1996 Holiday Catalog featured five cookie jars, one of which was glass, some with matching cookie plates.

Also, Coca-Cola, Mrs. Fields, Hershey, and Big Dog Sportswear have catalogs with at least one cookie jar. Check for web sites on the Internet or the 800 directory. Collectors have spoken: We like advertising cookie jars and their matching go-withs!

Row 1:   *Entenmann's Chef,* "MADE IN BRAZIL Exclusively for Entenmann's
1st Collector's Series/JCK 1992." $175.00 – 225.00

               Entenmann's Tractor-trailer die-cast model, "AHL *Mack* ©1991
HARTOY INC MADE IN CHINA." $18.00 – 22.00

               Quaker Graindrops, "WEISS HAND PAINTED MADE IN BRAZIL ©1981
THE QUAKER OATS CO." $175.00 – 225.00

Row 2:   *Katy the Korn Top Pig (Haeger),* embossed on top of lid, "BARTLOW
BROS. INC, KORN TOP," stamped in blue on bottom of foot "Haeger © USA."
A second example of Katy can be found embossed with "Schuyler Grain Co."
on the lid. The two jars are identical except for the logo. $90.00 – 110.00

               Haeger logo, foil label "Haeger® Floral MACOMB, IL." $18.00 – 22.00

Row 3:   *Big Dog* pepper shaker.   Issue price, set, $17.00

               Big Dog cookie jar, incised "BIG DOGS®, MADE IN THAILAND."   1996 issue price, $35.00

               Big Dog salt shaker.   Issue price, set, $17.00

Below: *MooTown Snackers,* unmarked. MooTown Snackers is a cheese
product distributed by Sargento Foods. $125.00 – 175.00

Row 1:   *Coke Jug*, brown top, "MADE IN THAILAND." $20.00 – 30.00

Coke Jug, green top, "MADE IN THAILAND." $20.00 – 30.00

Row 2:   *Coca-Cola Hollywood Polar Bear,* 2nd in the series. "Coca-Cola®
brand 1996 Limited Edition of 25,000 pieces HOLLYWOOD COOKIE JAR.
©1996 The Coca-Cola Company. All Rights Reserved." In addition,
"MADE IN PHILIPPINES" on small, gold label. $30.00 – 40.00

Always Cool Coke Polar Bear. On box, "You've seen him on TV
delighting fans in millions of dens across the country in the
Always Coca-Cola advertising campaign.
   "This is the one and only Coca-Cola Polar Bear. Lovable visitor
from the frozen north he's guaranteed to warm the home of any
family he joins." Apparently extremely successful, this one and only
Coca-Cola Polar Bear was joined by three additional examples by
the end of 1996. $25.00 – 35.00

Row 3:   *Coke Six-pack,* "Coca-Cola® © 1996, The Coca-Cola Company, All Rights
Reserved, Distributed by Enesco Corporation, Made in China."   Issue Price $65.00

Coke Machine, "Coca-Cola® © 1995, The Coca-Cola Company, All Rights
 Reserved, Distributed by Enesco Corporation, Made in China."   Issue Price $60.00

Below: *Polar Bear* in Santa hat and scarf, marked on bottom with transparent
decal and black lettering in oval, "AUTHORIZED COLLECTION Coca-Cola®
brand Cookie Jar Issue 1996." Then, "©1996, The Coca-Cola Company.
All rights reserved." On small, gold, oval, foil label "Made in Philippines."
   This jar was also offered with or without an ornament. It was easy to
differentiate; the jar without did not have a picture of the ornament on the
box.   Issue price with ornament $31.00

Polar Bear ornament. Marked with black lettering on transparent
label, "©1996, The Coca-Cola Company. All rights reserved." Small,
gold, rectangular, foil label reads "Made in Philippines."
                      Ornament price included in the price of the jar. Set, $31.00

Row 1: *Betty Crocker®* cylinder, "MADE IN TAIWAN, WELCOME INDUSTRIAL CORP." $80.00 – 90.00

Gulden's Mustard, glass, 12¼" high. $175.00 – 200.00

PB Max cylinder, "CANISTER 3½ QT, PFALTZGRAFF USA 506" $40.00 – 50.00

Row 2: *Sunshine Cookies & Crackers,* unmarked. $70.00 – 80.00

Kit Kat, incised into one side of jar "© CALIF FORMAL CLOCK CO." $275.00 – 325.00

Nabisco Foods Group cylinder, "USA." $35.00 – 45.00

Row 3: *Oreo* server, "THINK BIG! MADE IN USA" incised into the lid and the base of the cookie. $50.00 – 60.00

Stack of Oreo Cookies, "The Official Oreo cookie jar." In black lettering on the bottom of the base is "The Nabisco® Classics Collection ™ MADE IN CHINA." Issue price $29.95

Below: *Magic Oven* (Frankoma Pottery), "KEEBLER CO 1996" and Keebler Hollow Tree logo incised into bottom of base. $25.00 – 35.00

Chips Ahoy®™ cylinder, unmarked except for obvious logo. $35.00 – 45.00

Row 1: *Archway Van*, "MADE IN CHINA" on small foil, rectangular label. Advertised as "•High, luster ceramic • 10" L x 5¾" H •Not available in stores •Holds two packages of Archway cookies. •Only $15.95 and one proof of purchase." Issue price from Archway (available 1997) $15.95

Dubble Bubble Baseball, plastic, filled with Dubble Bubble chewing gum. $8.00 – 10.00

Row 2: *Big Boy*, "BIG BOY® EBR© 1996 SPECIAL 1996 LTD EDITION." Made in China. $100.00 – 125.00

US Soccer Ball, "Procter & Gamble, SPECIAL EDITION" in recognition of World Cup Soccer. Produced by Friendship Pottery, Roseville, Ohio. $35.00 – 45.00

Row 3: *Coffee Mug*, prototype, similar example approved for late 1997 release in a limited edition of 130 pieces. Paper label "Big Boy ® Elias Bros. Inc. Made by Wolfe Studio Michigan ©1977." Issue price $130.00

Below: *Big Boy,* 16" high, licensed replica of the 1956 Big Boy. Paper label, "Big Boy ® Elias Bros. Inc. Made by Wolfe Studio Michigan © 1997." Issue price $200.00

Row 1: *Television,* front and back sides, made by Treasure Craft for Nickelodeon to give as Christmas gifts to their employees. Each jar came with a certificate of authenticity. $500.00 – 600.00

Row 2: *Planet Hollywood* salt and pepper set. Small, oval label "MADE IN CHINA."   Issue price $12.00

Planet Hollywood cookie jar authorized by the unique restaurant chain owned by stars Bruce Willis, Demi Moore, Arnold Schwarzenegger, and Sylvester Stallone. Movie memorabilia is displayed and clips from movies are played for your entertainment while dining.   Issue price $28.00

Row 3: *Crayola Engine,* unmarked prototype never put into production though there are some samples around.   Price not determined.

Crayola Rocket, unmarked prototype never put into production though there are some samples around.   Price not determined.

Below: *Paradise Bakery Logo* cookie jar, made in Laguna Beach by Ken Auster in the late 80s – early 90s and featured in Christmas catalog. Only 100 jars were produced. Paradise Bakery's headquarters are located in Solona Beach, California. Flat, unglazed bottom; "Paradise" incised into surf board, barely visible on right. Guffey. $175.00 – 225.00

Major League Baseball was arranging production of *Baseball Bear* cookie jars and matching salt and pepper sets to be made for the teams. The Giants went so far as to advertise in their merchandise catalog. It is believed no more than four prototypes were made of any team, and only some of the teams are represented.

Row 1: *Dodgers,* Baseball Bear prototype by Certified International Corporation. Lytle. $400.00 – 450.00

Row 2: *Rockies,* Baseball Bear prototype by Certified International Corporation. Lytle. $400.00 – 450.00

Row 3: *Atlanta Braves,* Baseball Bear prototype by Certified International Corporation. Lytle. $400.00 – 450.00

Below: *Nestles Talking Bear,* mascot of Nestles refrigerated cookie dough. This is a replica of the *Talking Bear* Nestles used in television commercials. When this jar surfaced, Nestles was contacted. They totally denied its existence. We know it exists; how many more are there? Not enough samples have surfaced to accurately determine value. Dial.

Row 1:   *Nick at Nite* salt and pepper set, "©1997 VIACOM MADE IN CHINA."   Issue price $12.00

Row 2:   *Harrods* bank, "MADE IN ENGLAND BY JAMES SADLER & SONS LTD."
Martin   Issue price $60.00.

Below: *Hard Rock Hotel Bear,* "©LOTUS 1997 CHINA." Paper label "HANDCRAFTED
EXCLUSIVELY FOR LOTUS MADE IN CHINA."   Issue price $35.95

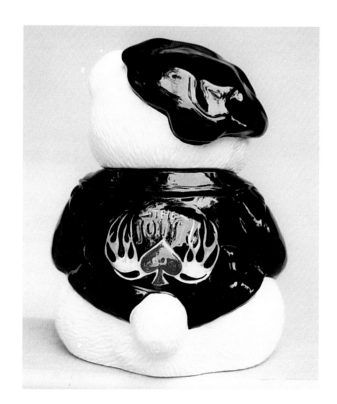

Row 1: *Special Angel* cookie jar, a Richard Simmons exclusive distributed through Fingerhut®. Transparent label "Richard Simmons." The cookie jar and salt and pepper set are part of an extensive Special Angel kitchen ware line. $50.00 – 60.00

Refrigerator and Special Angel salt and pepper set with certificate of authenticity. The certificate reads, "I believe that there are guardian angels looking over all of us, and I have carefully crafted my own special angels to watch over, inspire, and motivate you for a happy and healthy life." $15.00 – 18.00

Row 2: *Boy Face* coffee or tea cup, distributed by Bailey's Irish Cream liquor. Incised into bottom of base, "1996 Limited Edition." On small oval, gold-colored foil label, "Made in China."   Issue price of set, $14.95

Girl Face cookie jar, distributed by Bailey's Irish Cream liquor. Incised into bottom of base, "1996 Limited Edition." On small oval, gold-colored foil label, "MADE IN CHINA." Besides the pieces featured, there are a matching Boy Face cookie jar, Girl Face open sugar, Boy Face creamer, and Boy and Girl Face coffee pot or teapot. Issue price $24.95

Girl Face cup for coffee or tea, distributed by Bailey's Irish Cream liquor. Incised into bottom of base, "1996 Limited Edition." On small oval, gold-colored foil label "MADE IN CHINA."   Issue price of set $14.95

Row 3: *Sphinx* cookie jar, "Luxor, Las Vegas MADE IN THAILAND" impressed into bottom of base. $40.00 – 50.00

Egyptian motif, Luxor, Las Vegas, salt and pepper shakers.   Issue price $8.00 – 10.00

Mummy bank (composition), "Luxor Las Vegas" impressed into back. "MADE IN THAILAND" on rectangular, gold label. $25.00 – 35.00

Below: This photo shows the "Luxor, Las Vegas" mark on the cookie jar.

Row 1: *Chips Ahoy,* Cookie Keeper cylinder, unmarked except for obvious logo.
Issue price (Nabisco) $39.95

Row 2: *Keebler Sandies* cylinder, unmarked.
$70.00 – 80.00

Row 3: *Dreyer's Grand Ice Cream* cylinder, "CRAFTED WITH PRIDE™ IN USA©TREASURE CRAFT." The older version of Dreyer's Grand Ice Cream is shown in *Book II.*
$75.00 – 95.00

Below: *Badcock Cookies* cylinder, an incentive given by Badcock Furniture. Badcock is a furniture chain located in the southeastern part of the United States. There are two different Badcock cookie cylinders. The second version appears to be the same until you look at the fired-on decal on the bottom and see "Celebrating Our 89th Anniversary" (1993).
$25.00 – 35.00

Badcock Cookies logo on cylinders.

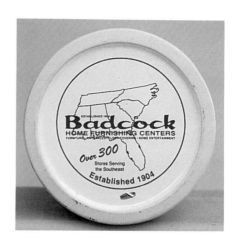

Row 1: *Hollow Tree,* embossed Keebler logo. Incised into bottom of base, "©KEEBLER CO. 1981." Manufactured by Friendship Potterty of Roseville, Ohio, circa 1993. Friendship was destroyed by fire mid-1996. $30.00 – 40.00

Hollow Tree cookie jar, logo on bottom of base. Though the copyright date is 1981, this is the newest of the three Keebler Hollow Tree cookie jars. This example was still available in 1997 through Sales & Market Service Associates of Rockford, Illinois.

Row: 2 The following Quaker Oats items could be bought only by Quaker Oats employees.

Mother's Oats trivet, "1995," Blackbird Pottery, Cedar Rapids, Iowa, plant. Oltmanns. $25.00 – 35.00

Mother's Oats utensil holder, "1995, 1 of 665." Oltmanns. $40.00 – 50.00

Mother's Oats cookie jar, 10" high, 3lbs. 7oz., manufactured by Blackbird Pottery, Amana, Iowa, "Spacek, Amana, IA, 1992, 1 of 950." Recipe, "*Mother's Oats* Bread 1½ cups *Mother's Oats* (uncooked), 2 teaspoons salt, 2 cups boiling water, 1 cake yeast, ½ cup sugar, ¼ cup lukewarm water, 5 cups flour. Mix together *Mother's Oats*, salt and sugar. Pour 2 cups of boiling water over mixture. Let stand until lukewarm, then add yeast which has been dissolved in ¼ cup lukewarm water, then add 5 cups of flour. Knead slightly, set in a warm place, let rise until light (about 2 hours). Knead thoroughly, form into 2 loaves and put in pans. Let rise again and bake about 50 minutes." This is an old Mother's Oats recipe from the time period before the name was changed to Quaker Oats. Oltmanns. $175.00 – 225.00

Mother's Oats milk pitcher, made in 1994, 1 of 600. Oltmanns. $40.00 – 50.00

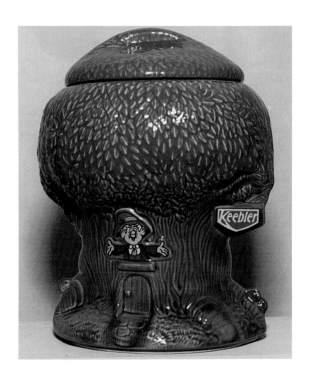

Row 1: *Montezuma* lamp, "OLMECA TEQUILA" on front. $50.00 – 60.00

Montezuma shot glass, "OLMECA TEQUILA" on front. $10.00 – 12.00

Montezuma cookie jar, believed to have been a sales incentive given by a liquor distributor during a certain time period. "OLMECA TEQUILA" on front, otherwise, unmarked. $150.00 – 175.00

Row 2: *Sun-Maid Raisins* cylinder, 8" high, "USA." Issue price $24.95

John Deere cylinder, 8" high, "USA." $30.00 – 40.00

Row 3: *President's Choice* cookie bag from which earthenware cookie jar was patterned.

President's Choice cookie bag, earthenware, "MADE IN CHINA." President's Choice brand originates in Canada. $120.00 – 130.00

Below: *Pharmaceutical* ginger jar, "©1975 DUNCAN CERAMICS INC." Niccum. $25.00 – 35.00

Row 1: *Grease Monkey,* unmarked. Armstrong. Not enough examples have surfaced to determine value.

KBPL (105.9) Watermelon Man, stamped, "Custom Made by ARTISTIC CERAMICS." Reed. Rare. Value not determined.

Row 2: *Mr. Peanut,* 10¼" high, "The Nabisco® Classics Collection™ MADE IN CHINA Distributed By Block® China Corporation for Nabisco, Inc." $35.00 – 45.00

Century 21, "©1994 CENTURY 21 REAL ESTATE CORP. MADE IN USA BY GOLD CREST, LTD. NO. HOLLYWOOD, CA." incised into back of building. A similar example is featured in *Book II* (the saying across the front is different). Guffey. $675.00 – 750.00

Row 3: *Ronald McDonald* bank, "MADE EXCLUSIVELY FOR MCDONALDS CORPORATION BY GROUP II COMMUNICATIONS, INC. HALES CORNERS, WI 53130 MADE IN TAIWAN, ©1993 MCDONALDS CORP." $35.00 – 45.00

Grimace bank, "MADE IN TAIWAN" on small, gold, rectangular foil label. Decal on back "GRIMACE®© 1985 McDonald's Corp. Thailand." $30.00 – 40.00

McDonald's Carry-out ceramic bank, "Made exclusively for GROUP II COMMUNICATIONS, INC. Holes Corners, WI 53130 Made in Thailand." $20.00 – 30.00

Ken-L-Ration Cat wall pocket, "F&F MOLD AND DIE WORKS INC., DAYTON, OHIO MADE IN USA." Azzam. $30.00 – 40.00

Ken-L-Ration Dog wall pocket, "F&F MOLD AND DIE WORKS INC., DAYTON, OHIO MADE IN USA." Azzam. $30.00 – 40.00

Ken-L-Ration Dog cookie jar, "F&F Mold and Die Works, Dayton, Ohio." Azzam. $120.00 – 140.00

Dog (Ken-L-Ration look-alike) bank, "Zadek Feldstein Co. Inc. N.Y.C." Azzam. $28.00 – 32.00

Ken-L-Ration Dog sugar bowl, unmarked. Azzam.   Set, $95.00 – 130.00

Ken-L-Ration Cat pepper shaker, "F&F Mold and Die Works, Dayton, Ohio." Azzam.   Set, $30.00 – 40.00

Ken-L-Ration Dog salt shaker, "F&F Mold and Die Works, Dayton, Ohio." Azzam.   Set, $30.00 – 40.00

Ken-L-Ration Cat creamer, unmarked. Azzam.   Set, $95.00 – 130.00

Row 1:   *Case Steam Engine,* "Commemorating the 150th Anniversary of J.I. Case Co., 1992 Limited Edition SERIAL#_____." On small, gold-colored, rectangular paper label "MADE IN R.O.C." $100.00 – 125.00

Mrs. Fields Chocolate Chip cookie jar, Niccum. $150.00 – 175.00

Row 2:   *The First Factory* holiday candy dish, 5½" high, "© 1992 HARLEY-DAVIDSON, INC." Small, gold colored, rectangular, foil label "MADE IN TAIWAN." $100.00 – 125.00

Children of the World, marked "Save the children® DANA — AGE 12 HELPING CHILDREN AND THEIR FAMILIES, CHINA."   Issue price $35.00

Row 3:   *Zep Manufacturing Drum,* Chemical Company. Unmarked. Phelps. $175.00 – 225.00

Kentucky Fried Chicken, glass (lampshade), unmarked. Robertson. $275.00 – 325.00

Below: *San Jose Sharks Goalie,* "____/100 WOLFE STUDIO COOKIE JAR ANTIQUES PRODUCTION LICENSED BY SAN JOSE SHARKS."   Issue price $125.00

Keitha, Keith in drag, (see page 21, *Book II*) "Cookie Jar Antiques Productions and Artist Candy E. Wynne – 1995.____/50 CW."   Issue price $200.00

36

Row 1:   *Doughboy* cylinder with glass lid (Anchor Hocking), unmarked. $12.00 – 18.00

Doughboy telephone sample, "© THE PILLSBURY CO., 1984 MADE IN HONG KONG." Working telephone, MIB. $300.00+

Doughboy cylinder with wooden lid (Anchor Hocking), unmarked. $12.00 – 18.00

Row 2:   *Pillsbury Best Flour Sack* cookie jar, Pillsbury Best All Purpose Flour (Benjamin & Medwin), in blue lettering, "BENJAMIN & MEDWIN INC. N.Y. N.Y., © 1993 T.P.C. MADE IN TAIWAN." $45.00 – 65.00

Pillsbury Best Flour Sack ceramic 3-piece canister set (Benjamin & Medwin), in blue lettering, "BENJAMIN & MEDWIN INC. N.Y., © 1988 T.P.C." Impressed into pottery, "BENJAMIN & MEDWIN INC. N.Y. N.Y© 1988 T.P.C." $60.00 – 75.00

Row 3:   Recipe on back of flour sack.

AMERICAN BISQUE COMPANY

The American Bisque Company of Williamstown, West Virginia, has wonderful coverage in *The Collector's Encyclopedia of Cookie Jars* and *Collector's Encyclopedia of Cookie Jars Book II*. With little doubt, American Bisque cookie jars are their most valuable asset, making them a natural for counterfeiters. The American Bisque licensed characters, Popeye, Olive Oyl, Swee' Pea, Casper, all the Flintstones, Baby Huey, along with the Mohawk Indian and Horse, have all been reproduced. We felt it was mandatory to measure and record accurate measurements to protect collectors and dealers. These measurements can be found in the 1997 update of *Book I*.

At least two different American Bisque cookie jars have surfaced with flat bottoms, no wedges. The commonly found or production pieces of these jars have wedges. Al Dye confirmed this was possible. Apparently the sculptor left the bottom flat, then a waste mold was made. Because Baby Huey and Casper were licensed pieces perhaps licensing approval was sought before fine tuning the piece and production molds were made. Another explanation might be that samples were cast to see how a finished piece would look and/or how much interest it would create.

Warning! There are Casper salt and pepper shakers on the market designed to blend with other American Bisque Casper pieces. These shakers are not American Bisque. It is believed, the basic Casper figure used for these 6" shakers were taken from an American Bisque Casper bank. These shakers, made by a Wisconsin ceramist, are not licensed.

Row 1: *Teakettle* (Martha and George) with image of young colonial couple embossed on side. Stamped in gold, "American Bisque Co. USA 22kt gold." $40.00 – 50.00

Row 2: *Dutch Shoe*, 5" high, 10" long, unmarked. Rare. Horelica. Price not determined.

Row 3: *Hen with Chick,* multicolored, 8⅞" high, 9½" long, "USA." Horelica. $125.00 – 150.00

Below: *Casper*, prototype, "©HARVEY-1961 USA," 13½" high. The commonly found Casper is marked, "©Harvey Productions, Inc. USA" (see page 42, *Book I*). Zimmerman. Price not determined.

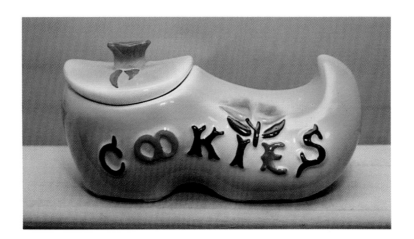

Row 1:   CJ-560 Assortment
               Floral CJ-561 $30.00 – 35.00
               Chest CJ-562 $150.00 – 175.00
               Recipes CJ-563 $90.00 – 110.00

Row 2:   CJ-750 Assortment
               French Poodle CJ-751 $100.00 – 125.00
               Grandma CJ-752 $100.00 – 125.00
               Jack-in-Box CJ-753 $125.00 – 150.00

Row 3:   *Puppy* CJ-754 $60.00 – 70.00
               Lady Pig CJ-755 $70.00 – 90.00
               Churn CJ-756 $25.00 – 35.00

Below: CJ-700 Assortment
               Bear CJ-701 $50.00 – 60.00
               Chick CJ-702 $100.00 – 125.00
               Pig CJ-703 $70.00 – 90.00

COOKIE JARS

CJ-700 ASSORTMENT

BEAR   CHICK   PIG

COOKIE JARS

CJ-560 ASSORTMENT

FLORAL
CJ-561

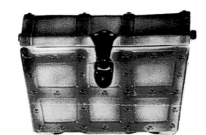

CHEST
CJ-562

RECIPES
CJ-563

CJ-750 ASSORTMENT

FRENCH POODLE
CJ-751

GRANDMA
CJ-752

JACK IN BOX
CJ-753

PUPPY

LADY PIG

CHURN

APPLEMAN

A partial showing of the works of Glenn Appleman is featured in *Book II*. Appleman cookie jars continue to gain acclaim among collectors, both cookie jar and automotive. The inspiration for Glenn Appleman's cookie cars came directly from his youth. The most important cultural event from 1950 to 1959 was the yearly unveiling, and subsequent appearance around the neighborhood, of the fabulous, new car models. In those days, there was no restraint or boring clean lines; everything was chrome, fins, and two-tone pastels. These cars were practically family members. Teens spent their weekends in them going to the beach, they held flashlights long into the night while their fathers desperately tried to get those new oil filters in place; they jumped all over the parked cars on the street until the owners came and chased them away.

Looking back, Glenn felt as if car designers were out to appeal directly to him, a kid growing up in the Bronx. It might have been America's love affair with the automobile that kept him in business from 1978 to 1987, but it was his love for cars that made his cookie jars beautiful. Appleman's professional creativity and quality have never been duplicated.

Row 1:   *Jaguar XK-140 Convertible,* one of 12 made in green, gray, black, or red. There is one white Jaguar. Honchar. $1,750.00 – 2,000.00

Row 2:   *Corvette,* an Appleman favorite, based on the 1959 Corvette. Approximately 900 were made from June 1985 until July 1987 in red with white trim, white with red trim, and black with white trim. Originally retailed for $450.00. $1,000.00

Row 3:   *Stingray* (burgundy) prototype, privately commissioned. $5,000.00

Below: *Antonio the Mechanic.* Though mounted on a mahogany base, this is actually a cookie jar. Though originally conceived as a production piece it proved too difficult to make. Honchar. $5,000.00

Row 1:   *Sudzo*, an excellent example of custom work done on the Rolls Royce line. Various owners of Rolls Royces frequently commissioned special glazing or ornamentation. The standard *Rolls,* usually in red and black or gray and black, originally sold for $600.00. A few standard Rolls were produced in yellow and black; brown/tan and burgundy/gray are the hardest colors to find in a standard Rolls. The *Rolls Royce* line was completed in 1987 with final production numbers of approximately 1,000 pieces. $2,000.00

Row 2:   *Humperbump Woody Convertible*, one of six pieces produced, each done in a different color. $1,500.00

Row 3:   *Vegetable Truck with Gorilla*, top opening. Most examples had gold lettering on the sides reading "Vito's Veggies." Approximately 25 pieces were made of this Appleman Autoworks production piece. Originally retailed for about $500.00. $2,500.00

Below: *I Shall Return*, General Douglas MacArthur in green Packard convertible. One-of-a-kind. $4,000.00

      Dewey Defeats Truman created in 1982 for a public television auction. In 1985 about eight more were made. $2,500.00

Row 1:   *Buick Convertible,* created in 1981, discontinued 1987. Available in red, white, black, brown, and green. $1,000 .00

Row 2:   *Phantazoom,* created in 1981, based on several cars with big fins from the late fifties. *Phantazooms* are mostly two-tone with a pink body and gray inset. $1,000.00

Row 3:   *Packard Convertible,* created in 1979. Idea taken largely from a 1939 Packard Coupe. Available in red, white, brown, black, and green. $1,000.00

Below: *Alfred Hitchcock* caricature, one of a kind. In artist's collection. $5,000.00

   Chairman Mao Tse-tung, one of a kind. Charles Joseph. $7,500.00

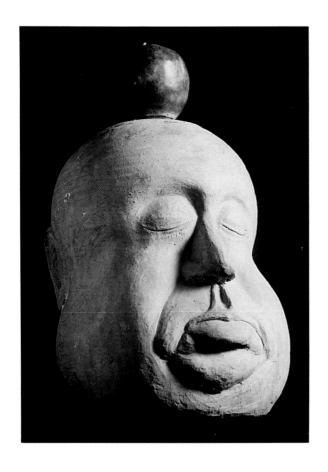
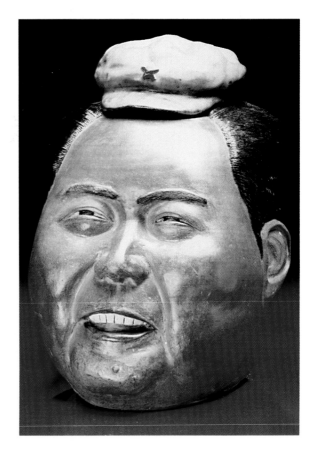

BLACK AMERICANA

Black Americana remains a top collectible among cookie jars. Because Black Americana is sought after by other than cookie jar collectors, competition heightens demand. Because of their collectibility, many have been reproduced (See the Reproduction chapter for some examples). For additional, extensive coverage of Black Americana, see *The Collectors Encyclopedia of Cookie Jars, Books I and II.*

Row 1: *Mammy,* 9½" high, "ARTISTIC POTTERIES INC. CALIF – USA – 31."
Stamped in brown, "HAND PAINTED CALIFORNIA." Horelica. $625.00 – 675.00

Chef, 10½" high, ARTISTIC POTTERIES – INC. CALIF – 30." Horelica. $425.00 – 475.00

Mammy, 9½" high, "ARTISTIC POTTERIES INC. CALIF – USA – 31."
Horelica. $525.00 – 575.00

Row 2: *Boy with Watermelon* humidor. Heyrman. $800.00+

Mammy covered sugar bowl, "JAPAN." $225.00 – 275.00

Row 3: *Maid and Butler* salt and pepper set, Brayton Laguna Pottery,
5" and 5⅜" high, unmarked. Horelica. $475.00 – 525.00

Maid, Brayton Laguna Pottery, 12¾" high, "© Brayton Laguna
Pottery." Horelica. $1,500.00+

Below: *Mammy,* hard plastic, "F & F Mold & Die Works,
Dayton, Ohio." This jar was placed on public display at the first
annual National Cookie Jar Show for the enjoyment of all. Rare.   Price not determined.

Mammy, hard plastic, "F & F Mold & Die Works,
Dayton, Ohio." Burkett. Rare.   Price not determined.

Row 1: *Mammy* (Nanna reproduction), 11" high, marked "WD 40 USA,"
distributed by Maurice Ceramics. $25.00 – 35.00

Calypso Mammy, "MADE IN INDONESIA" on a small, oval paper label. $40.00 – 50.00

Mammy (Nanna reproduction), 11" high, marked "WD 40 USA,"
distributed by Maurice Ceramics. $25.00 – 35.00

Row 2: *New Mama* creamer, on transparent label blue "S" under a crown,
and "MADE IN INDONESIA" on a small, oval paper label. Not
a Mandy reproduction though the designs are similar.   Set $35.00 – 45.00

New Mama cookie jar (similar to OCI's *Mandy*, but not a reproduction),
on transparent label blue "S" under a crown, and "MADE IN INDONESIA"
on a small, oval paper label. $60.00 – 70.00

New Mama covered sugar bowl, on transparent label blue "S" under a
crown, and "MADE IN INDONESIA" on a small, oval paper label.   Set $35.00 – 45.00

Row 3: *African Village* clock, unmarked. Offered through Avon in 1996.
Our grandson, Herndon Joseph, added the clock to Grandma's
African Village set, Christmas 1996. $25.00 – 35.00

African Village salt and pepper, unmarked, 1½" high. Offered
through Avon in 1996.   Set $18.00 – 22.00

African Village cookie jar, "MADE IN CHINA" on small gold-colored
paper label. 8" high x 6½" wide. Offered through Avon in 1996. $40.00 – 45.00

Below: *Original Cookie Doll* (Beloved Belinda) cookie jars by Renita Pines,
limited edition.   Issue price $250.00

Row 1: *Black Americana Santa* cookie jar. Marked on bottom of jar with black back stamp, "a la carte J C Penney styles for the home. Made in China. Hand wash only. Not Recommended for use in a Microwave Oven." Issue price $24.99

Santa plate and mug. "a la carte J C Penney styles for the home. Made in China. Hand wash only. Not Recommended for use in a Microwave Oven." Plate marked identically. Set $16.99

Row 2: *African-American Mrs. Santa* candy jar, 8⅛" high, "© OCI 1993." Paper label, "OCI TAIWAN." Issue price $49.00

African-American Santa and Christmas Tree salt and pepper set, "© OCI 1993." Paper label, "OCI TAIWAN." $18.00

Row 3: *African-American Mrs. Claus* cookie jar, 10" high, "© OCI 1993." Paper label, "OCI TAIWAN." Issue price $77.00

Mrs. Claus creamer and *Christmas Tree* sugar bowl, "© OCI 1993." Paper label, "OCI TAIWAN." Set $31.50

Below: *Santa Head*, "_____/50 WOLFE STUDIO Made For COOKIE JARS ET CETERA." $50.00 – 60.00

54

Row 1: *China Mammy,* unmarked, china body, imported from China, mid-90s. Available in two sizes, this is the large size. $60.00 – 70.00

Mammy, McCoy reproduction. China body, imported from China. $30.00 – 40.00

Row 2: *Mammy,* unmarked, unknown. Williams. $60.00 – 70.00

Mexico Mammy, unmarked, available with yellow, green, or blue dress. $70.00 – 80.00

Mexico Mammy tool holder, available with yellow, green, or blue dress. $30.00 – 35.00

Row 3: *Santa* (Scioto mold), "An Original Sculpture by Don Winton." $275.00 – 325.00

Santa, back view (Scioto mold), "An Original Sculpture by Don Winton." $275.00 – 325.00

Below: *Grand Marshal,* "GRAND MARSHAL Mardi Gras Records©, ©1995 MADE IN THE U.S.A. BY TREASURE CRAFT ____OF 500 LIMITED EDITION OLYMPIA BRASS BAND." This is the original *Grand Marshal.* A second *Grand Marshal* jar has been produced by Clay Art for Mardi Gras Records. $175.00 – 225.00

Mammy, Brayton reproduction, transparent label, "E. Stewart Collection 1992." Betsey's Collectibles. $30.00 – 40.00

Row 1: *Ragtime,* "CLAY ART SAN FRANCISCO COOKIE JAR, RAGTIME ©1995 CLAY ART, HAND PAINTED, MADE IN CHINA." Incised into bottom of base "C.A."   Issue price $50.00

Amazing Grace, "CLAY ART SAN FRANCISCO COOKIE AMAZING GRACE ©1995 CLAY ART, HAND PAINTED, MADE IN CHINA." Incised into bottom of base "C.A."   Issue price $35.00

Row 2: *Jazz Player,* "CLAY ART SAN FRANCISCO COOKIE JAR, JAZZ PLAYER ©1995 CLAY ART, HAND PAINTED, MADE IN CHINA." Incised into bottom of base "C.A."   Issue price $35.00

Row 3: *Baking Time,* "CLAY ART SAN FRANCISCO COOKIE JAR, BAKING TIME ©1995 CLAY ART, HAND PAINTED, MADE IN CHINA." Incised into bottom of base "C.A."   Issue price $35.00

Below: *Jazz Player* salt and pepper set, "C.A." incised. Paper label "Clay Art Made In China."   Issue price $15.50

Rag Time salt and pepper set, "C.A." incised. Paper label "Clay Art Made In China."   Issue price $15.50

Baking Time salt and pepper set, "C.A." incised. Paper label "Clay Art Made In China."   Issue price $15.50

Memories of Mama®
™Treasures From the Heart

The works of Diane Goodin were introduced in *Book I.* Diane's first originals, Savannah and Lee Roy, are featured in *Book II* with additional items from the Ora and Thelma lines.

Row 1: *Thelma,* four piece canister set, "MEMORIES OF MAMA® *diAnn* TULSA OK." There is a full kitchenware line available for Diane's Sunflower and Watermelon lines: sugar and creamer, salt and pepper, jam jar, spoon caddy, napkin holder, and fruit jar covers.   Issue price for 4-piece canister set, $270.00

Row 2: *Noel* (Angel) cookie jar, "MEMORIES OF MAMA® NOEL© 1997 DIANE GOODIN TULSA, OK PROTOTYPE 3."   Issue price $300.00

Row 3: *Thelma,* four piece canister set, "MEMORIES OF MAMA® *diAnn* TULSA OK."   Issue price for 4-piece canister set, $270.00

Below: *Modena,* snapping beans, cookie jar, "MEMORIES OF MAMA® ©1997 DIANE GOODIN *diAnn* TULSA, OK #____."   Issue price $175.00

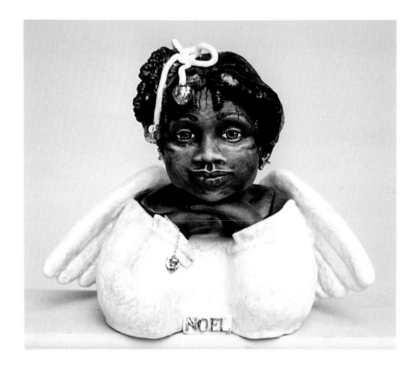

The New Rose Collection

The New Rose Collection and previous works (The Collection of Rose) were introduced in *Book II*. The New Rose Collection continues to grow with private contract work and the creation of outstanding originals. Rose commissioned Don Winton to sculpt the official jar for the 1998 National Cookie Jar Show as well as former Regal China artist (the creator of *Cookie Jarrin's Little Angel*) to produce a limited edition Tucker car for Lark Creations. Both jars are featured in *Book III*.

Row 1:   *John Henry* cookie jar, a character from US folklore. "TNRC (and number)." Discontinued.   Issue price $135.00

Cotton Ginny cookie jar, limited edition of 100, "TNRC."   Issue price $125.00

Row 2:   *Santa,* "TNRC Rose & Gary Saxby," 8¾" high. $50.00 – 60.00

Tiger salt or pepper shaker. Incised into bottom "3." The palm tree separates into two pieces, one half for salt, the other pepper.   Issue price, set $45.00

Sambo & Tiger cookie jar, "#___/of 250."   Issue price $150.00

Sambo salt or pepper shaker. Incised into bottom, "3." The palm tree separates into two pieces, one half for salt, the other pepper.   Issue price, set $45.00

Row 3:   *Martin Luther King, Jr.* salt or pepper shaker.   Issue price $50.00

Martin Luther King, Jr. cookie jar, stamped, "TNRC."   Issue price $175.00

Martin Luther King, Jr. salt or pepper shaker.   Issue price $50.00

The Dream, "By the NEW ROSE COLLECTION TNRC." Discontinued. Issue price $135.00

Below: *Mammy* utensil holder (Crackpot commercial mold). Also available in red. Unmarked.   Issue price $25.00

Mammy and Chef (small) salt and pepper set (Crackpot commercial mold). Also available in red. Unmarked.   Issue price $17.00

Mammy signature cookie jar (Crackpot commercial mold), also available in red. "Rose Saxby."   Issue price $55.00

Mammy bell (Crackpot commercial mold), also available in red. Unmarked.   Issue price $17.00

Chef and Mammy (large) salt and pepper set (Crackpot commercial mold), also available in red. Unmarked.   Issue price $25.00

Watermelon Girl cookie jar, "The New Rose Collection 100 limited edition No.____."   Issue price $135.00

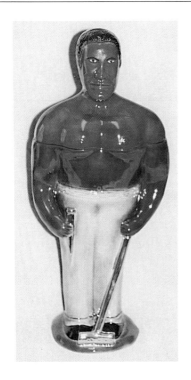

JC MILLER

The works of JC Miller were introduced in *Book II.* Besides the jars featured on these two pages, the Millers produced the official jar for the third annual National Cookie Jar Show, a "Nashville or Bust" Pick-up.

Row 1: *Sister Ruth* cookie jar, "___/250." On card: Sister Ruth, singing praise on Sunday morning is where you will find Sister Ruth. She is regal in her blue choir robe with a yellow bow at her neck. She is hand painted and trimmed in 22 kt. gold. Clarice Bell Miller."
Issue price $49.00

Sister Ruth salt and pepper set, 6" high.
Issue price $125.00

Row 2: *Andrew McClellan,* incised "JC Miller" "___/100" written in black under glaze. First in a collection of military figures. History as it appears on card: "Andrew McClellan was born in North Carolina in 1839, on the George McClellan plantation. He enlisted in the United States Infantry, Regiment 13, Company C, August 31, 1863, at Estill Springs, Tennessee.
"Andrew received an honorable discharge as Corporal, January 1, 1866. He was just one of more than 200,000 African-American enlisted men who fought in the Civil War. Model by Clarice Bell Miller. Number 1 in Military Collector Series."
Issue price $125.00

Shilbogee Turry-Weery incised "JC" with "Miller" inside the C and number "___/100" written in black under glaze. Family history on accompanying card: "Shilbogee was born an African Prince, later being sold to a Captain Gilmore of Massachusetts. His name was changed to Tobias Gilmore.
"Tobias enlisted as a private in 1776. At one time he served as one of General George Washington's body guards. Model by Clarice Bell Miller. Number 2 in Military Collector Series."
Issue price $125.00

Row 3: *Sarah.* On story card: "Sarah Ann Saxton was born in Nashville, TN, in 1868. Her family moved to Kansas where she met and married George A. Douglas. They moved to Oklahoma during the land rush of 1889 and settled outside Hennessy, where she was a member of the local Baptist church. She was the mother of six children."
Issue price $95.00

Cora and George, signed in script "Cora & George ___/250." Family history on accompanying card: "Cora was born in Oklahoma Territory in 1890. She was the eldest child of Sarah. George, who is being held by his sister, was born in 1898. He was the youngest child of Sarah." Model by Clarice Bell Miller.
Issue price $120.00

Right: *Mystery Woman,* "JC "Miller" incised "___/100" in black under the glaze. Enclosed card reads: "MYSTERY WOMAN...is a young woman I met at a local ice cream store. She has a warm pleasant personality as well as being attractive. I asked her to model for a cookie jar and possibly a painting. She was willing, but disappeared before I learned her full name." Model sculpted by Jerry P. Miller.
Issue price $125.00

McMe Productions

The Meyers' first cookie jar, the *Bell Captain,* is featured in Black Americana in *Book II.*

Row 1: *Uncle Justin* (yellow hat), "McMe" in the shape of a heart, then "©93, LIMITED ED NO ____500, So. Calif."   Issue price $90.00

Uncle Justin (red hat), "McMe" in the shape of a heart, then "©93, LIMITED ED NO ____500, So. Calif." Though the mark indicates differently, the *Uncle Justin* (wearing red hat) is not a numbered series.   Issue price $90.00

Row 2: *Florence Mildred,* "McMe" within heart, "Produced by McMe Productions Simi Valley CA Made in U.S.A. Florence Mildred ____/250." This is a prototype; dress color will be different on the production pieces.   Issue price $125.00

Additional cookie jar creations by Gerald and Lona Meyer can be found under McMe.

Paul Hoadley

Clown cookie jar by Paul Hoadley (Nashport, OH), "#___1996 Paul S Hoadley."   Issue price $75.00

Shipman Pottery

Row 3: *Jamimah,* Shipman Pottery (Post, TX), "JAMIMAH '92 ___/300." Model decorated by Rose Saxby (New Rose Collection).   Sample, price not determined.

BRUSH

The Brush Pottery of Zanesville, Ohio, began production in 1906. After manufacturing for less than one year, the pottery burned. George Brush leased the Crooksville Clay Products Company and stored what pottery, molds, etc., he had been able to salvage. He became manager of the Globe Stoneware Company selling his wares through a catalog carrying the company name, Zanesville-Crooksville Sales Company.

George Brush joined McCoy in 1909. On August 24, 1911, he bought the former J. B. Owens Plant No. 1. In October of 1911, Brush offered to sell his molds, saggers, catalogs, and real estate to J. W. McCoy. The offer was accepted November 7, 1911. On December 13, 1911, the stockholders voted unanimously to change the name of the J. W. McCoy Pottery Company to The Brush-McCoy Pottery Company which continued through 1925.

On December 9, 1925, the stockholders decided to resolve the articles of incorporation of The Brush-McCoy Pottery Company and to amend the name to The Brush Pottery Company, because the McCoy family had sold their interest in Brush-McCoy in 1918. (In 1910, J. W. McCoy founded The Nelson McCoy Sanitary Stoneware Company in Roseville, Ohio, with his son, Nelson McCoy, Sr. After J. W. McCoy's death December 11, 1914, Nelson McCoy continued to represent his family in Brush, serving as a member of the directorate until he resigned in 1918.)

The earliest figural cookie jar manufactured by Brush is the *Elephant with Monkey Finial.* The production date is listed as 1946 in Huxford's *The Collector's Encyclopedia of Brush McCoy Pottery.* This was 21 years after the resolution of Brush-McCoy. The trademark registration of McCoy instituted by Roger Jensen was challenged by Designer Accents owner, Ralph Porto. From that point Jensen began marking his product, "Brush-McCoy." It is important to remember, if a jar marked Brush-MCoy is new, it probably is a reproduction. All the figural Brush jars known and loved today were manufactured by Brush after the dissolution of Brush-McCoy. It is confusing when books on Brush-McCoy Pottery include cookie jars. The pottery manufactured by and marked Brush-McCoy is highly collectible; any figural cookie jar marked Brush-McCoy is not.

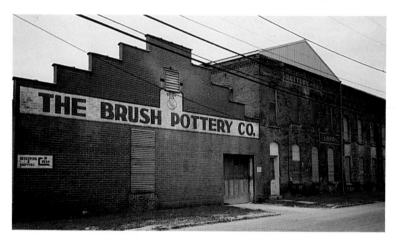

Row 1:   *Lady in Blue,* unmarked but confirmed Brush. Moloney. $3,500.00

            Cow with Cat Finial, blue with gold trim, "W 10 USA." Moloney. $2,000.00 – 2,500.00

Row 2:   *Fish,* unmarked, unusual cobalt blue accent. Eggert/Seman.   Priced not determined.

            Humpty Dumpty (with beanie and bow tie), gold trim, "W 18 Brush USA." Moloney. $400.00 – 500.00

Row 3:   *Little Boy Blue,* rare prototype with "LITTLE BOY BLUE" incised into pottery above right foot. Firestone.   Price not determined.

CALIFORNIA CLEMINSONS

California Cleminsons was founded in 1941 by George and Betty Cleminson at their home in El Monte, California. The Cleminsons' business venture outgrew the confines of their garage, making expansion necessary.

Cleminsons' lively Pennsylvania Dutch style is highly acclaimed and sought after by collectors today. Their artware was all hand-decorated underglaze with colored slip (liquefied clay). Additional examples of Cleminsons are featured in *Book I* and *Book II*. The *House*, featured in *Book II*, is the common version. There is another, plainer version with a gingerbread-man shape and round cookies on the roof.

Row 1:   *Coffeepot* wall pocket, "THE CALIFORNIA CLEMINSONS Cb HAND
PAINTED ©." $35.00 – 45.00

King, 10½" x 8", "THE CALIFORNIA CLEMINSONS Cb." Andrews. $500.00 – 550.00

Row 2:   *Pennsylvania Dutch* (motif) cookie canister, part of brown Distlefink
dinnerware line. Though away from the norm, Betty
Cleminson was fond of flower finials; it is possible this lid is original.
"The California Cleminsons© Hand painted." Candee. $70.00 – 80.00

Galagray cookie canister, "THE CALIFORNIA CLEMINSONS
Cb galagray Ware ©." Wooldridge. $75.00 – 90.00

Potbellied Stove, 9" x 6½", "THE CALIFORNIA CLEMINSONS Cb © HAND
PAINTED." Wooldridge. $175.00 – 225.00

Pennsylvania Dutch (motif) canister, "The California Cleminsons ©
Hand painted." Wooldridge. $70.00 – 80.00

Row 3:   *Pig,* hard to find, "THE CALIFORNIA CLEMINSONS Cb © HAND
PAINTED." Wooldridge. $225.00 – 275.00

Cookstove, "THE CALIFORNIA CLEMINSONS Cb © HAND
PAINTED." Wooldridge. $150.00 – 175.00

Numerous variations of Cleminsons' *King* have surfaced. To be certain of authenticity, look for the Cleminsons' stamp under the glaze.

Below: This backstamp was used
on the rare rose-colored
Potbellied Stove and
Cookies cylinder.

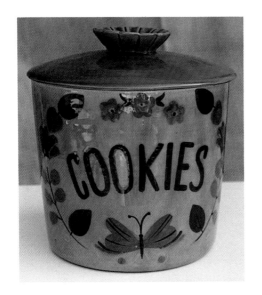

CHARACTERS AND PERSONALITIES

Characters are the cornerstone of collecting. Cookie jar collectors are not the only ones interested in character products. For example, the Sesame Street character Elmo skyrocketed to fame when Rosie O'Donnell, taking a cue from her son, introduced the "Tickle Me Elmo" doll on her show. Enesco should have presented Ms. O'Donnell with an *Elmo* cookie jar.

Characters are feel-good collectibles. We can relive our childhood while capturing the interest of our children and grandchildren (the future collectors). The selection of banks, salt and pepper shakers, telephones, figurines, etc., is endless. It is our good fortune to be collectors during this era with the revival of older characters being at an all-time high. When Turner Entertainment merged with Warner Brothers, the production of character cookie jars was greatly accelerated. Turner now had access to vast vaults of characters once owned exclusively by Warner Brothers.

Many famous personalities from our youth are back: Marilyn Monroe, James Dean, Elvis Presley, Laurel and Hardy, the Three Stooges, Hopalong Cassidy, Gene Autry, Roy Rogers, and Dale Evans. All have been immortalized in cookie jars. We refuse to let these memories fade. The race is on to capture audiences of all ages, in all mediums.

Additional characters and personalities can be found in Happy Memories, McMe Productions, Star Jars, etc., plus Walt Disney and the Warner Brothers chapters. It is important to know many of the older character jars have been reproduced; some are featured beside the original in the reproduction chapter. Collectors that collect only characters can amass an enormous variety, but characters are a cross collectible making competition greater for that special "got-to-have" piece.

Row 1: *50th Anniversary Smokey Bear* cookie jar, "SMOKEYS 50TH ANNIVERSARY OFFICIAL LICENSEE • COOPERATIVE FOREST FIRE PREVENTION PROGRAM AUTHORIZED BY 18 U.S.C. 711 1944–1994 Made in U.S.A. Cookie Jarrin' © 1994 Mfg. by Treasure Craft 'ONLY YOU CAN PREVENT FOREST FIRES' Original Sculpture by Don Winton." Limited Edition of 450. $400.00 – 500.00

Smokey Bear full-bodied bank, "OFFICIAL LICENSEE COOKIE JARRIN' © 1996 Authorized by 16 USC 580 P-4."   Issue price $49.95

Smokey Bear bank, "USA" back of pants. Rare. Posner. $750.00

Row 2: *Smokey Bear* two-piece salt and pepper set (head one shaker, hat the other). "OFFICIAL LICENSEE COOKIE JARRIN' © 1996 Authorized by 16 USC 580 P-4."   Issue price $39.95

Smokey Bust cookie jar, "9 Out Of 10 Forest Fires Are Caused By People OFFICIAL LICENSEE COOPERATIVE FOREST FIRE PREVENTION PROGRAM AUTHORIZED BY 18 U.S.C. 711 Made in U.S.A. Cookie Jarrin' © 1995 Mfg. by Treasure Craft #____Remember, Only You Can Prevent Forest Fires."   Issue price $89.95

Smokey Bear head bank, "COOKIE JARRIN' © 1996 OFFICIAL LICENSEE MADE IN THE USA AUTHORIZED by 16 USC 580 P-4."   Issue price $29.95

Wendy the Good Little Witch limited edition cookie jar, "Wendy the Good Little Witch™ © 1996 Harvey Comics, Inc. A Harvey Entertainment Company. All Rights Reserved. Licensed by MCA/Universal Merchandising, Inc. Licensed to – *Cookie Jarrin'* Original Sculpture by Don Winton."   Issue price $169.00

Row 3: *Smokey Bear* cookie jar, unmarked. This jar has been found with both a totally flat, bare pottery bottom with wedges on the base. Rare. Davis. $1,750.00 – 2,000.00

Smokey Bear cookie jar, unmarked. Rheinheimer. $1,750.00 – 2,000.00

The United States Forest Service (USFS) is adamant about it, but does it really make a difference? The controversy over Smokey's "middle" name does not die. The fact is that Smokey "the" Bear was approved and licensed by the USFS as early as 1952 when the Ideal Toy Corporation produced the first official product, a plush bear. Other companies receiving licenses to promote Smokey "the" Bear products included Little Golden Books, Big Golden Books, Whitman Publishing Company, Dell Comic Books, Peter Pan Records, and Columbia Record Company. In early 1952, Hill & Range Songs was granted a license to write the song, "Smokey the Bear." From 1957 through 1960, Smokey the Bear comic strips were distributed to newspapers nationwide.

It seems that sometime during 1959 a decision was made to drop Smokey's unofficial "middle" name. Why? No one in the Forest Service knows except to state, "His name is Smokey Bear." In May 1952, the Smokey Bear Act was passed by Congress establishing Smokey's legal name as "Smokey Bear." Products licensed since 1960 reflect the correct name. Notable exceptions are items licensed prior to 1960 such as the Golden Books and the music by Hill & Range, which were permitted to still use Smokey the Bear. In 1966, the *Ballad of Smokey the Bear*, narrated by James Cagney, was produced for television's General Electric Theater based upon the Hill & Range song.

Once in a while, the old name manages to pass by the USFS. In 1976 the R. Dakin Company produced a 6.75 inch vinyl Smokey with the name Smokey the Bear. Ironically, all the other Dakin products made from the early 1970's through 1985 were licensed with the Smokey Bear name. A Junior Forest Ranger badge, first seen in 1989, has the words "Smokey the Bear" embossed on it.

Obviously, the use of "the " in Smokey's name shouldn't be that big of a deal, although no one likes being called by a wrong name. It has been said that there is no "the " in Mickey Mouse or even in Big bird to show that there should not be a "the" in Mickey Mouse or even in Big bird to show that there should not be a "the " in Smokey's name either. But we can not forget "Frosty the Snowman," "Kermit the Frog," "Rudolph the Red Nosed Reindeer," or even "Clarabelle the Clown," all equally famous personalities.

So whether you call him "Smokey the Bear," "Smokey Bear," or just plain "Smokey," he is still dear in our hearts and very collectible. Richard Yokley, *Hot Foot Teddy News* 1 October 1995.

Row 1: *Smokey Bear* papier-maché bank, unmarked Norcrest. Dial. $125.00 – 150.00

       Smokey Bear candy jar (one of three styles), "Norcrest." Dial. $225.00 – 275.00

Row 2: *Smokey Bear* ashtray, "Norcrest." Dial. $100.00 – 125.00

       Smokey Bear bank, unmarked. Dial. $225.00 – 275.00

Row 3: *Smokey Bear* bank, "B. P. Import Japan" on paper label. Dial. $125.00 – 175.00

       Smokey Bear bank, "NORCREST Crafted in Japan Reg US Pat Off A-478." Dial. $275.00 – 300.00

Right: *Smokey Bear* candy or biscuit jar, "USA." Dial. $500.00+

Smokey Bear music box, Norcrest. Darrow. $325.00 – 375.00

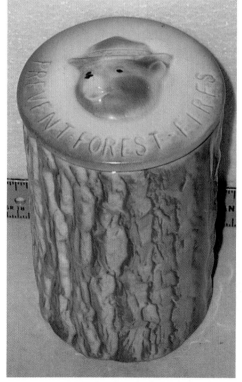

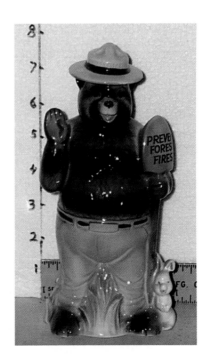

Row 1: *Snoopy Doghouse,* "BENJAMIN & MEDWIN INC. N.Y.N.Y., ©'58 '66 UFS, MADE IN TAIWAN." $30.00 – 40.00

Snoopy telephone (small, lying down), "F.C.C., #C447NP-11358-MT-E, RINGER EQUIVALENCE NUMBER 0.4B, U.S.O.C. JACK CODE RJ11." $35.00 – 45.00

Snoopy plastic bank, in fine print below "CHEX PARTY MIX AND PEANUTS 40 YEARS OF TRADITION, PEANUTS Characters ©1950, 1952 United Features Syndicate, Inc." On back, "©1950, 1958, 1965, 1966 United Feature Syndicate, Inc." On bottom, "MADE IN CHINA." $5.00 – 8.00

Row 2: *Charlie Brown,* stamped in black under glaze, "BENJAMIN & MEDWIN INC. N.Y.N.Y., ©'52, '66 UFS, INC., MADE IN TAIWAN." $35.00 – 45.00

Joe Cool Snoopy telephone, label on bottom of base reads, "TRADE NAME SEIKA, MODEL NO.: SNOOPY PHONE SLK-291, COMPLIES WITH PART 68, FCC RULES FCC REGISTRATION NO.:1ZHCHN-65372-TE-E, RINGER EQUIVALENCE AC 2.1B, DC 1.8, U.S.O.C.: RJ11C, LISTED ETL®. S09910KTCOC, SEIKA, MADE IN CHINA." $40.00 – 50.00

Lucy, stamped in black under glaze, "BENJAMIN & MEDWIN INC. N.Y.N.Y., ©'52, '66 UFS, INC., MADE IN TAIWAN." $35.00 – 45.00

Row 3: *Snoopy Pilot,* "WORLD WAR I FLYING ACE: flying behind enemy lines, searching for the Red Baron's triplane, Snoopy looks danger in the eye.
"Clad in a leather flying helmet, scarf, and goggles, he can also be spotted on leave, taking time out for a root beer in a French bistro and trying out phrases from his French/English dictionary on local lasses." Stamped in black under glaze, "BENJAMIN & MEDWIN INC. NEW YORK, N.Y., PEANUTS ©United Feature Syndicate, Inc., MADE IN CHINA." $35.00 – 45.00

Snoopy on Hot Dog bank, "SNOOPY: 1958, 1966 United Feature Syndicate, Inc." $20.00 – 25.00

Snoopy with Red Bow, stamped in black under glaze, "BENJAMIN & MEDWIN INC. NEW YORK, N.Y., PEANUTS ©United Feature Syndicate, Inc., MADE IN CHINA." $30.00 – 35.00

Below: *Snoopy* plastic bank, used in Christmas campaign for Whitman's. $5.00 – 8.00

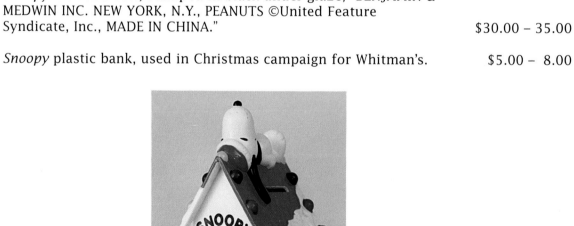

Row 1: *Shining Time Station,* "Schmid ©Quality Family Entertainmnent, Inc. 1994." Paper label, "CAUTION! This is NOT a toy, NOT recommended for children under the age of three (3) Without parental supervision." A second paper label, "Schmid, Sri Lanka." Descriptive story on box: "Deep in the heart of the Indian Valley, just East of Daydream Mountain and West of Mount Tomorrow, lies Shining Time, a small town — population 5,006 give or take. Shining Time exemplifies the American Dream: family, community, hard work, and neighborly townsfolk.

The bustling whistle stop, at the heart of the community, was built in 1885 and is now known as Shining Time Station — the oldest stop on the Indian Valley Railroad.

Through the always open doors you'll find fun, enchanting stores and the zaniest group of townsfolk this side of Doodlehaven. Anything is possible at Shining Time as long as you believe in magic!

Come find out why people say 'There is just something about this place.'

This Shining Time Station is brought to you by Schmid, a world leader in fine gifts and collectibles since 1932." Britt™ (Britt Allcroft). $60.00 – 70.00

Thomas the Tank Engine lamp, © Britt Allcroft (Thomas) LTD 1989. "MADE IN TAIWAN" on paper label. $25.00 – 35.00

Thomas the Tank Engine & Friends™ (as seen on Shining Time Station), "Schmid, ©Britt Allcroft (Thomas) Limited 1994." On paper label, "Schmid, SRI LANKA." Descriptive story: "Thomas is a cheeky, fussy little engine. He often gets into scrapes, usually by being over-eager to do things best left to bigger and more sensible engines. But clouds never last long in Thomas' life and he's soon bustling about again, playing his part in the yard and on his very own branch line, of which he is extremely proud." $60.00 – 70.00

Row 2: *Big Bird in Fire Truck* savings bank, "1993 © Jim Henson Productions, Inc., LICENSEE ENESCO CORPORATION, Made in China." Paper label, "CAUTION, THIS IS NOT A CHILD'S TOY." $20.00 – 25.00

Elmo in Train Engine savings bank, "1993 © Jim Henson Productions, Inc., LICENSEE ENESCO CORPORATION, Made in China." $25.00 – 30.00

Big Bird with Book night light, "1993 Jim Henson Productions, Inc., LICENSEE ENESCO CORPORATION, Made in China." Paper label, "CAUTION, THIS IS NOT A CHILD'S TOY." $38.00 – 42.00

Row 3: *Elmo,* "CTW SESAME STREET® 1994 © Jim Henson Productions, Inc. LICENSEE ENSECO CORPORATION MADE IN CHINA" on a transparent label that could easily be removed. A second white paper label, "CAUTION – THIS IS NOT A CHILD'S TOY." $50.00 – 60.00

Cookie Monster, "1993 © Jim Henson Productions, Inc., LICENSEE ENSECO CORPORATION Made in China" on a transparent label that could easilay be removed. "CAUTION – THIS IS NOT A CHILD'S TOY." $50.00 – 60.00

Thomas the Tank Engine light switch plate, "BRITT ALLCROFT (THOMAS) LIMITED 1992 MFG. BY HAPPINESS EXPRESS INC. MADE IN CHINA." On back, "PATENT PENDING HAPPINESS EXPRESS INC. MADE IN CHINA." $8.00 – 10.00

Thomas the Tank Engine plastic lamp, "MFG. BY HAPPINESS EXPRESS INC. MADE IN CHINA 120 volts ac 60 hz E127539 MFG #7." On side of track, "©BA (T) LIMITED.1992." $10.00 – 15.00

Row 1: *Superman bank,* transparent label, "TM & © DC COMICS INC. 1987, LICENSEE ENESCO IMPORTS CORP., MADE IN TAIWAN ROC." Small, gold-colored, rectangular paper label, ENESCO™ DESIGNED GIFTWARE, ©1987 ENESCO IMPORTS INC., MADE IN TAIWAN R.O.C." $50.00 – 60.00

Superman cookie jar, paper label reads, "DESIGNED EXCLUSIVELY FOR THE WARNER BROS. STUDIO STORE, MADE IN CHINA. ™ & © WARNER BROS. 1997." Impressed into bottom of base, "D.C. COMICS, ™ & © 1997, MADE IN CHINA."   Reissued $40.00

Superman telephone, issued by Allied Telecommunications in California, "ATE Serial No, 1265 FCC Reg. No. BC 686F-67491-TE-R Ringer Equivalence 1.OA Complies with Part 68 FCC Rules Superman Rotary Model TM & © D.C. COMICS 1981." $350.00+

Row 2: *Batman* high-impact plastic coin bank, from the animated series, marked "Distributed By Kid Dimension Made in China, © 1994 DC Comics, Inc. All Rights Reserved." FYI: "Batman swoops down from the sky in pursuit of street thugs and his evil arch enemies! The Caped Crusader™ never tires of capturing criminals and protecting law-abiding citizens." $8.00 – 10.00

Batman soft plastic bank, "TM & © 1994 DC Comics, Inc." $8.00 – 10.00

Batman hard plastic bank, "TM & © 1995 DC Comics." $8.00 – 10.00

Batman cookie jar, "TM & © DC COMICS, MADE IN CHINA." $125.00 – 150.00

Row 3: *Spider-man* telephone, "SPIDER-MAN™ © 1994 MCG MADE IN HONG KONG." $40.00 – 50.00

Spider-man plastic bank a Spider-man cereal box premium, "Manufactured by STREET KIDS, Los Angeles, CA 90016 Copyright © 1991, Marvel Entertainmebnt Group, Inc., All Rights Reserved." $8.00 – 10.00

Spider-man cookie jar prototype, unmarked, never produced.

     Value not established.

Below: *Batmobile* telephone, "©1995 DC COMICS ©1995 MICRO GAMES OF AMERICA ALL RIGHTS RESERVED MADE IN CHINA." Paper label, "BAT-8040 MANUFACTURED IN CHINA COMPLIES WITH PART 68 FCC RULES FCC REG NO: BSYCHN-22444-TE-E REN#:0.7B USED STANDARD JACK: USOC RJ11C." $65.00 – 75.00

Row 1:   *Yoshi* musical cookie jar (Welcome Industries Corp.), "COPYRIGHT TM & ©
1993 NINTENDO, ALL RIGHTS RESERVED" on transparent label.
"MADE IN TAIWAN" on small, gold-colored, rectangular label. $35.00 – 45.00

Princess Toadstool, Princess of the Mushroom Kingdom musical
cookie jar (Welcome Industries Corp.), "COPYRIGHT TM & © 1993
NINTENDO, ALL RIGHTS RESERVED" on transparent label. "MADE
IN TAIWAN" on small, gold-colored, rectangular label. $35.00 – 45.00

Mario musical cookie jar (Welcome Industries Corp.), "COPYRIGHT TM & ©
1993 NINTENDO, ALL RIGHTS RESERVED" on transparent label.
"MADE IN TAIWAN" on small, gold-colored, rectangular label. $35.00 – 45.00

Row 2:   *Doctor Mario* musical bank (Welcome Industries Corp.), "COPYRIGHT TM & ©
1993 NINTENDO, ALL RIGHTS RESERVED" on transparent label.
"MADE IN TAIWAN" on small, gold-colored, rectangular label. $18.00 – 22.00

Toadie musical cookie jar (Welcome Industries Corp.), "COPYRIGHT TM & ©
1993 NINTENDO, ALL RIGHTS RESERVED" on transparent label.
"MADE IN TAIWAN" on small, gold-colored, rectangular label. $35.00 – 45.00

Luigi musical bank (Welcome Industries Corp.), "COPYRIGHT TM & ©
1993 NINTENDO, ALL RIGHTS RESERVED" on transparent label.
"MADE IN TAIWAN" on small, gold-colored, rectangular label. $18.00 – 22.00

Row 3:   *Yoshi* musical bank (Welcome Industries Corp.), "COPYRIGHT TM & ©
1993 NINTENDO, ALL RIGHTS RESERVED" on transparent label.
"MADE IN TAIWAN" on small, gold-colored, rectangular label. $18.00 – 22.00

Mario telephone, "DIALFONE LIMITED., TELEPHONE MBS-38 COMPLIES
WITH PART 68 FCC RULES, FCC REGISTRATION NUMBER, CEV8EDJ-2127-TE-E,
RINGER EQUIVALENCE, REQUIRED CONNECTOR: USOC RJ11C,"
and "NINTENDO OF AMERICA INC. © 1990." $30.00 – 40.00

Bowser, King of the Koopa musical bank (Welcome Industries
Corp.), "COPYRIGHT TM & © 1993 NINTENDO, ALL RIGHTS RESERVED"
on transparent label. "MADE IN TAIWAN" on small, gold-colored,
rectangular label. $18.00 – 22.00

Row 1:   *Raggedy Ann,* "©1993 MACMILLAN, INC, CERTIFIED INT., TAIWAN." $75.00 – 95.00

Raggedy Andy, "©1993 MACMILLAN, INC, CERTIFIED INT., TAIWAN." $75.00 – 95.00

Row 2:   *Lambchop* plastic lamp, "©1993 SHARI LEWIS ENTERPRISES, INC.," Bottom
of base, "MFG. BY HAPPINESS EXPRESS INC. MADE IN MACAU 120 volts
ac 60 hz E127539 MFG #3." $10.00 – 12.00

Lambchop plastic bank, "©1993 SHARI LEWIS ENTERPRISES, INC., MANUF
BY H.E.I. MADE IN CHINA" around rim of base. "MADE IN CHINA." $10.00 – 12.00

Raggedy Andy, "1972 THE BOBBS-MERRILL CO. LIMITED"
under glaze. The matching Raggedy Ann is featured in *Book II,*
page 137, bottom right. $325.00 – 375.00

Row 3:   *Felix the Cat,* "BENJAMIN & MEDWIN INC. N.Y.N.Y., ©1991 FELIX THE
CAT PRODUCTIONS, INC., MADE IN TAIWAN." Discontinued. $40.00 – 50.00

Lambchop, not marked. Shari Lewis' Lamp Chop & Friends, distributed
by Benjamin & Medwin. $45.00 – 55.00

Betty Boop, stamped under glaze "BENJAMIN & MEDWIN INC.,
NEW YORK, N.Y., 1995 King Features Syndicate, Inc./Fleischer
Studios, Inc., ™The Hearst Corporation, MADE IN CHINA." $30.00 – 35.00

Row 1: *James Dean*, "TM/© 1996 James Dean Foundation
by CMG World wide, Indianapolis, IN 46202 USA. Designed and
Distributed Exclusively by Clay Art. MADE IN CHINA." Incised into
bottom of base "C.A."   Issue price $60.00

Marilyn Monroe, "TM/© 1996 The Estate of Marilyn Monroe
All Rights Reserved, Licensed by CMG Worldwide, Indianapolis,
IN 46202 USA. Designed and Distributed Exclusively by Clay
Art. MADE IN CHINA." Incised into bottom of base "C.A."   Issue price $60.00

Row 2: *Lucy Glamour Box*, stamped under glaze "© VANDOR
1996 CHINA." Paper label, "I Love Lucy is a REG. TM of CBS Inc.
Images of Lucille Ball & Desi Arnaz are used with the permission of
Desilu, too. Licensing by Unforgettable Licensing. Sculpted by
Preston Willingham for VANDOR, SLC UT • MADE IN CHINA."   Issue price $36.00

Forever Friends mug, incised "©VANDOR 1996 CHINA." Fired-on
decal, "I Love Lucy" in red heart. "I LOVE LUCY is a REG. TM of CBS
Inc. Images of Lucille Ball & Desi Arnaz are used with the permission
of Desilu, too. Licensing by Unforgettable Licensing. Sculpted by
Preston Willingham for VANDOR, SLC UT • MADE IN CHINA."   Issue price $15.00

Lucy Chocolate Factory salt and pepper set incised "© VANDOR
1996 CHINA." Paper label "I Love Lucy is a REG. TM of CBS Inc. Images
of Lucille Ball & Desi Arnaz are used with the permission of Desilu,
too. Licensing by Unforgettable Licensing. Sculpted by Preston Willingham
for VANDOR, SLC UT • MADE IN CHINA."   Issue price $26.00

Lucy Vitameatavegamin wall clock, paper label "I Love Lucy is a REG.
TM of CBS Inc. Images of Lucille Ball & Desi Arnaz are used with the permission
of Desilu, too. Licensing by Unforgettable Licensing. Sculpted by
Preston Willingham for VANDOR, SLC UT • MADE IN CHINA."   Issue price $26.00

Row 3: *Portrait Bank*, incised "©VANDOR 1996 CHINA." Fired-on
decal "I Love Lucy" in red heart. "I LOVE LUCY is a REG. TM of CBS Inc.
Images of Lucille Ball & Desi Arnaz are used with the permission of Desilu,
too. Licensing by Unforgettable Licensing. Sculpted by Preston
Willingham for VANDOR, SLC UT • MADE IN CHINA."   Issue price $30.00

I Love Lucy cookie jar, incised, "©VANDOR 1996 CHINA." Fired-on
decal, "I Love Lucy" in red heart. "I LOVE LUCY is a REG. TM of CBS Inc.
Images of Lucille Ball & Desi Arnaz are used with the permission of
Desilu, too. Licensing by Unforgettable Licensing. Sculpted by
Preston Willingham for VANDOR, SLC UT • MADE IN CHINA."   Issue price $150.00

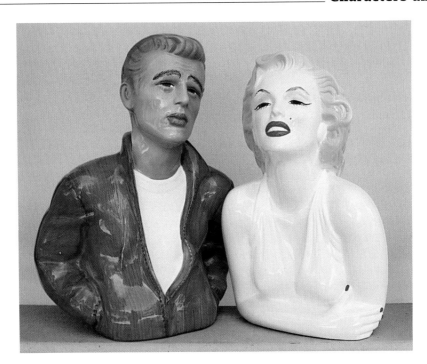

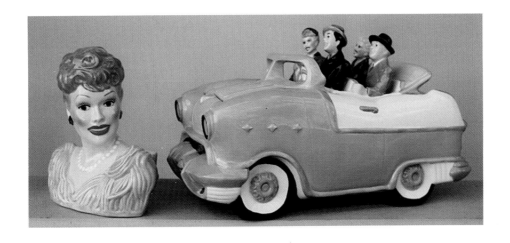

Row 1: *Cowardly Lion* bank, "©1939 LOEW'S INCORPORATED, REN. 1966
METRO-GOLDWYN-MAYER INC., ©1988 TURNER ENTERTAINMENT
CO. ALL RIGHTS RESERVED LICENSEE ENESCO IMPORTS CORP. MADE
IN TAIWAN ROC." Paper label, "ENESCO™ DESIGNED GIFTWARE ©1989
ENESCO IMPORTS CORP. MADE IN TAIWAN R.O.C." $40.00 – 50.00

Tin Man bank, "©1939 LOEW'S INCORPORATED, REN. 1966
METRO-GOLDWYN-MAYER INC., ©1988 TURNER ENTERTAINMENT
CO. ALL RIGHTS RESERVED LICENSEE ENESCO IMPORTS CORP. MADE
IN TAIWAN ROC." Paper label, "ENESCO™ DESIGNED GIFTWARE ©1989
ENESCO IMPORTS CORP. MADE IN TAIWAN R.O.C." $50.00 – 60.00

Scarecrow bank, "©1939 LOEW'S INCORPORATED, REN. 1966
METRO-GOLDWYN-MAYER INC., ©1988 TURNER ENTERTAINMENT
CO. ALL RIGHTS RESERVED LICENSEE ENESCO IMPORTS CORP.
MADE IN TAIWAN ROC." Paper label, "ENESCO™ DESIGNED
GIFTWARE ©1989 ENESCO IMPORTS CORP. MADE IN TAIWAN RO.C." $40.00 – 50.00

Row 2: *Clay Art* catalog sheet:
1951 Dorothy Mask.   Issue price $50.00
1952 Tin Man Mask.   Issue price $50.00
1953 Scarecrow Mask.   Issue price $50.00
1954 Cowardly Lion Mask.   Issue price $50.00
1955 Dorothy/Scarecrow and Lion/Tin Man salt and pepper. $28.00 – 32.00
1957 Napkin holder. $35.00 – 40.00
1956 Witches salt and pepper. $28.00 – 32.00

Below:. *Wizard of Oz,* "THE WIZARD OF OZ" across back of base. "USA" incised
into bottom. "Rick Wisecarver No. — 95 RS" on back of lid. Limited
availability, no longer in production. $325.00 – 375.00

Additional Wizard of Oz cookie jars can be found in the Star Jars chapter.

THE WIZARD OF OZ

DOROTHY

THE SCARECROW

THE TIN MAN

THE COWARDLY LION

Clay Art captures the wonder and magic of Oz. Collectable ceramic masks, salt and peppers and a napkin holder are all licensed exclusively with Turner Home Entertainment. These wonderful products are sure to catch the collector's eye. All products are gift boxed.

DOROTHY MASK	**1951**
TIN MAN MASK	**1952**
SCARECROW MASK	**1953**
COWARDLY LION MASK	**1954**

NAPKIN HOLDER **1957**

SALT & PEPPER (4 characters) **1955**

SALT & PEPPER (witches) **1956**

Salt and Peppers sold separately.

Row 1:   *Goldilocks and Three Bears,* JC Penney, "THE HOME COLLECTION MADE IN TAIWAN." $32.00 – 38.00

Mary Had a Little Lamb, JC Penney, "THE HOME COLLECTION MADE IN TAIWAN." $32.00 – 38.00

Three Little Kittens, JC Penney, "THE HOME COLLECTION MADE IN TAIWAN." $32.00 – 38.00

Row 2:   *Humpty Dumpty,* JC Penney, "THE HOME COLLECTION MADE IN TAIWAN." $32.00 – 38.00

Three Little Pigs, JC Penney, "THE HOME COLLECTION MADE IN TAIWAN." $32.00 – 38.00

Old Woman in Shoe, JC Penney, "THE HOME COLLECTION MADE IN TAIWAN." $32.00 – 38.00

Row 3:   *Mother Goose Bus,* "Walls Reg. U.S. Pat. Off. MADE IN JAPAN" on round label. $475.00 – 525.00

Below: *Cinderella,* basket handle cracker jar. Import. Divine. $800.00

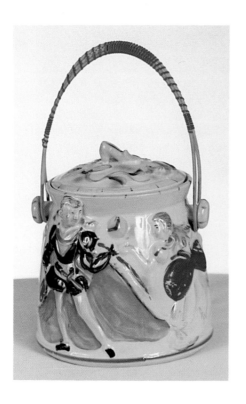

Row 1: *Benjamin Franklin,* "Made exclusively for Strawbridge & Clothier
By Treasure Craft A PFALTZGRAFF COMPANY NO — LIMITED EDITION
OF 1000 PCS." Original issue, fewer than 500 of the 1000 jars were
actually produced. $175.00 – 275.00

Uncle Sam, "©1995 A&B AMERICAN COOKIE JAR CO. —OF 150 1995
MADE IN USA." Comes with certificate of authenticity that states, "A&B
American Cookie Jar Company believes that our cookie jars should
be detailed and imaginatively sculpted. Each hand-crafted piece
will be treasured for generations to come.
   "Discover the beautiful patriotic cookie jar collection. Each jar will
bring out the heritage of the American legend."
   Certificate of Authenticity: "It is certified that this collectible
Number ____/150 is an authentic, handpainted limited edition design for A&B
American Cookie Jar Company. This design is issued in a strictly limited
edition of 150 after which this design will not be copied. The one-of-a-kind
master mold will be destroyed to preserve the integrity of the edition.
Design number 1, Design Name Uncle Sam (signed by) President/CEO
A&B American Cookie Jar Company." NOT A REPRODUCTION!   Issue price $150.00

Sneagle, Great American Cookie Company, small, oval, gold-colored
label, "MADE IN CHINA." $40.00 – 50.00

Row 2: *Droopy Dog*™ (Tex Avery's) manufactured by Treasure Craft for James
Morrison and John DeSalvo d.b.a. Animation. Limited edition
500 numbered/25 promotional. Only 150 cookie jars of
Droopy Dog were actually produced by Treasure Craft for
Animation. "ANIMATION *Droopy Dog.* This is a strictly limited edition
of 500 pieces. Your number is____ ©TURNER HOME ENTERTAINMENT
MADE IN U.S.A." $325.00 – 375.00

Nancy, "USA POTTERY BY JD. NANCY NO ___ UNITED FEATURE
SYNDICATE INC." $150.00

Nancy, full-bodied, "POTTERY BY JD. NANCY NO ___ UNITED
FEATURE SYNDICATE INC." $200.00

Row 3: *Sweet Pickles Alligator* (front and back), "SWEET PICKLES ™ & © 1981 Euphrosyne
Inc. Licensee Enesco Inc." On gold foil label, "Enesco design giftware
Korea." DiRenzo. $125.00 – 175.00

Hilda Hippo, transparent label on bottom "Richard Scarry's VERY BEST
EVER © 1988 Richard Scarry." Distributed exclusively by Goebel
United States. $100.00 – 125.00

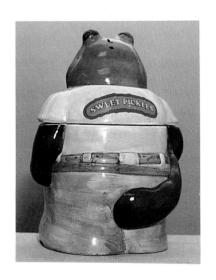

Row 1: *Dino and Pebbles*, bank, "©HANNA-BARBERA PRODUCTIONS INC., LICENSED BY HAMILTON PROJECTS." Paper label, "MADE IN JAPAN." Note, this bank is marked and colored differently than the example featured in *Book II*. The one in *Book II* is the first bank released by Vandor and is identified with only a paper label. This is their second bank, and probably the most common. A third variation is marked simply with an incised, "Made in Japan" no indication of licensing, and is the lightest in coloring. $70.00 – 80.00

Fred and Pebbles salt and pepper set, "©H.B.P.I. C.I.C. CHINA."   Set $18.00 – 22.00

Dino and Pebbles cookie jar, stamped, bottom of base, "© HANNA BARBERA PRODUCTION INC. CERTIFIED INTERNATIONAL CORP. CHINA." $45.00 – 55.00

Row 2: *Barney Rubble* cookie jar, stamped, bottom of base, "©HANNA BARBERA PRODUCTION INC. CERTIFIED INTERNATIONAL CORP. CHINA." $45.00 – 55.00

Fred and Barney Lodge Brothers salt and pepper set, "©H.B.P.I. C.I.C. CHINA."   Set $18.00 – 22.00

Flintstone cookie jar (cylinder), stamped, "1994 H.B.P.I. CERTIFIED INTERNATIONAL CORP MADE IN TAIWAN." $45.00 – 55.00

Row 3: *Fred Flintstone* cookie jar, "© HANNA BARBERA PRODUCTION INC. CERTIFIED INTERNATIONAL CORP. CHINA." $45.00 – 55.00

Fred and Dino salt and pepper set, "©H.B.P.I. C.I.C. CHINA."   Set $18.00 – 22.00

Flintstone House cookie jar, stamped "© HANNA BARBERA PRODUCTION INC. CERTIFIED INTERNATIONAL CORP. CHINA." $45.00 – 55.00

Row 1:   *Barney Rubble* canister, "1994 HBPI CERTIFIED INTERNATIONAL
CORP. MADE IN TAIWAN." $20.00 – 25.00

Fred Flintstone canister, "1994 HBPI CERTIFIED INTERNATIONAL
CORP. MADE IN TAIWAN." $20.00 – 25.00

Pebbles canister, "1994 HBPI CERTIFIED INTERNATIONAL CORP.
MADE IN TAIWAN." $20.00 – 25.00

Dino canister, "1994 HBPI CERTIFIED INTERNATIONAL CORP.
MADE IN TAIWAN." $20.00 – 25.00

Row 2:   *Fred Flintstone* plastic fruit snack container, "The Flintstones™ ©1994
HBPI FRED FLINTSTONE Mfg. by Ferrara Pan Candy Co. Forest Park,
IL 60130 USA." $15.00 – 18.00

Fred Flintstone cookie jar. A mold was made from a fruit sack container,
then decorated by Denise Teeters. Marked in black under glaze, "___/200,
D '94."   Issue price $150.00

Fred Flintstone plastic fruit snack container, "The Flintstones™ ©1994
HBPI FRED FLINTSTONE Mfg. by Ferrara Pan Candy Co. Forest Park,
IL 60130 USA." $15.00 – 18.00

Row 3:   *Fred and Dino* plastic lamp, "© 1982 Hanna-Barbera Prod. Inc." Darrow. $10.00 – 12.00

Dino bank, England. "© 1990 Hanna-Barbera Productions Inc. An
exclusive Harry James Design®™." $70.00 – 80.00

Fred Flintstone figurine, England. Marked as above. $30.00 – 35.00

Below: *Fred and Barney* figurines, "©1990 HBP inc." On box, "Special Limited
Edition figurines Compliments of Post®, VANDOR SALT LAKE
CITY, UTAH." Never distributed.   Price not determined.

Betty Rubble face mug, "©VANDOR 1990." Paper label, "©1990
HANNA-BARBERA PRODUCTIONS, INC. LICENSED BY HAMILTON PROJECTS,
INC." Small, oval, gold-colored foil label "MADE IN KOREA." $15.00 – 20.00

Row 1:   *Kermit with Fish Bowl,* "Henson Treasure Craft Made in China" incised
into bottom of base.   Issue price $50.00

Kermit phone, "KERMIT THE FROG™ PHONE ©1983 HENSON ASSOCIATES
INC. MADE IN SINGAPORE. model no teif 8030, part no 205059-02,
mfg code 8504, COMPLIES WITH PT 68, FCC RULES FCC REG. NO.
AA499C-68899-TE-T, Ringer Equivalence 0.9B American ATC,
Telecommunications Corporation A Comdial Company EL MONTE,
CA 91731." $175.00 – 225.00

Miss Piggy, "Henson Treasure Craft Made in China" incised into the
bottom of the base. The same mark, much smaller, is incised under
her arm where the lid comes off.   Issue price $50.00

Row 2:   *Fozzie,* "Henson Treasure Craft Made in China" incised into
bottom of base.   Issue price $50.00

Kermit serenading Miss Piggy, stamped on unglazed flat bottom,
©HENSON MEXICO." Incised under lid, "©HENSON TREASURE
CRAFT." Stamped on unglazed area under lid, "MEXICO." Discontinued. $65.00 – 75.00

Miss Piggy against column, stamped on unglazed flat bottom, "©
HENSON MEXICO." Incised under lid, "© HENSON TREASURE CRAFT."
Stamped on unglazed area under lid, "MEXICO." Discontinued. $65.00 – 75.00

Row 3:   *Big Bird* cylinder, "505." $35.00 – 45.00

Cookie Monster cylinder, "U.S.A. DEMAND MARKETING HENDERSON,
KY. MADE IN U.S.A. ©MUPPETS INC." $35.00 – 45.00

Ernie, Bert, and Cookie Monster cylinder, jar itself not marked, character
decal, "Muppet Characters © 1980 Muppets, Inc." $35.00 – 45.00

Below: *Big Bird, Bert, and Ernie* cylinder, "U.S.A. DEMAND MARKETING
HENDERSON, KY. MADE IN U.S.A. © MUPPETS INC." $35.00 – 45.00

Kermit candy jar, "Sigma the Tastesetter © HENSON ASSOC." $150.00 – 165.00

Row 1: *Waldorf and Statler* bookends, "©Sigma the Tastesetter ©HENSON ASSOC." $250.00 – 300.00

Kermit face mug, "©Sigma the Tastesetter ©HENSON ASSOC." $12.00 – 15.00

Kermit telephone, "TELEMANIA™ T 0796 MODEL: KERMIT TELEPHONE COMPLIES WITH PART 68 FCC RULES FCC NO: EMWCHN-61762-TE-E RINGER EQUIVALENCE: 1.1B U.S.O.C: RJ11C MADE IN CHINA." White paper label, "ETL LISTED ®87095 KERMIT TELEPHONE TELEPHONE EQUIPMENT KCL TECHNOLOGY LIMITED. GC QC PASSED." Issue price $50.00

Miss Piggy mug, "©Sigma the Tastesetter ©HENSON ASSOC." $12.00 – 15.00

Row 2: *Dr. Honeydew and Beaker in TV* (small) canister (3-piece set), incised "©Sigma the Tastesetter ©HENSON ASSOC." Large, green paper label, "A JIM HENSON MUPPET™ hand painted ceramics Sigma the Tastesetter." On small, oval label "MADE IN JAPAN." $225.00 – 275.00

Kermit in TV cookie jar, incised, "©Sigma the Tastesetter ©HENSON ASSOC." Large, green paper label "A JIM HENSON MUPPET™ hand painted ceramics Sigma the Tastesetter." $375.00 – 425.00

Miss Piggy (large) canister (3-piece set), incised, "©Sigma the Tastesetter ©HENSON ASSOC." Large, green paper label "A JIM HENSON MUPPET™ hand painted ceramics Sigma the Tastesetter." $275.00 – 300.00

Old Men in Balcony (medium) canister (3-piece set), incised "©Sigma the Tastesetter ©HENSON ASSOC." Large, green paper label "A JIM HENSON MUPPET™ hand painted ceramics Sigma the Tastesetter." $225.00 – 275.00

Row 3: *Waldorf* egg cup, "©Taste Setter Sigma..." on paper label. $50.00 – 75.00

Sam (the eagle) egg cup, "©Taste Setter Sigma..." on paper label. $50.00 – 75.00

Statler egg cup, "©Taste Setter Sigma..." on paper label. $50.00 – 75.00

Row 4: *Miss Piggy* on egg-shaped covered box, "©Taste Setter Sigma PLEASE NOTE THAT ALL PIECES ARE HAND DECORATED, SO COLOR VARIANCES COULD OCCUR. LABORATORY TESTED TO COMPLY WITH FDA GUIDELINES MADE IN JAPAN" on paper label. A copyright symbol is barely visible under the paper label. $75.00 – 85.00

Miss Piggy heart-shaped box, "©Sigma the Tastesetter ©HENSON ASSOC." $45.00 – 65.00

Miss Piggy bud vase, "©Sigma the Tastesetter ©HENSON ASSOC." $40.00 – 60.00

Gonzo sugar bowl, "©Sigma the Tastesetter ©HENSON ASSOC." $60.00 – 75.00

Fozzie Bear mug, "©Sigma the Tastesetter ©HENSON ASSOC." $25.00 – 30.00

Miss Piggy teapot, "©HENSON ASSOC." Paper label reads "©Taste Setter Sigma PLEASE NOTE THAT ALL PIECES ARE HAND DECORATED, SO COLOR VARIANCES COULD OCCUR. LABORATORY TESTED TO COMPLY WITH FDA GUIDELINES MADE IN JAPAN" $150.00 – 200.00

Viacom

Row 1: *Phaser Type II,* 3-piece salt and pepper set from original Star Trek™ series. Made exclusively for the Viacom Entertainment Store™.   Suggested retail $18.00

Mighty Mouse and Pearl (Terrytoons™) salt and pepper shakers, dolomite. Made exclusively for the Viacom Entertainment Store™. "©sigma the tastesetter HENSON ASSOC."   Suggested retail $16.00

Row 2: *Tommy Pickles* (Rugrats) cookie jar, "©1996 VIACOM CREATED BY KLASKY/CSUPO.   Suggested retail $40.00

Phil & Lil Deville (Rugrats) salt and pepper shakers, dolomite. Made exclusively for the Viacom Entertainment Store.   Suggested retail $18.00

Welcome to the world of Nickelodeon™ Rugrats™, an animated series about life from a baby's point of view. The Rugrats are one-year-old Tommy and his friends, Chuckie, Phil & Lil, and his cousin Angelica. Whenever adults are around, the Rugrats act like real babies; but, when they're alone, they drop their witless pose and talk to each other with the vocabulary of five-year-olds. As Tommy and his pals wobble through life supported by legs not yet used to walking, they show us the world as a baby views and understands it. The Rugrats' world is one that exists below our knees; here, mundane things and events turn into grand, comic adventures.

Rugrats is a sophisticated show for today's sophisticated children. Instead of talking down to its audience, it assumes children are intelligent and discriminating viewers. And, though children aged 6 through 12 are the primary target audience, *Rugrats* appeals to the 2–5 age group as well as to adults.

Rugrats was created by Arlene Klasky, Gabor Csupo, and Paul Germain. The series is written and produced by Klasky Csupo, Inc. in conjunction with Nickelodeon.

Row 3: *Real Monsters* cookie jar, "© 1996 VIACOM CREATED BY KLASKY/CSUPO MADE IN CHINA."   Issue price $36.00

AAAHH! Real Monsters. Deep beneath a smelly garbage dump, in a city very much like your own, a generation of promising young monsters is growing up. Ickis, Oblina, and Krumm are students in one of the world's elite monster academies, where they're studying the fine art of scaring the daylights out of people. Learning to be a top monster from their strict headmaster, The Gromble, is hard work. The trio relies on each other's help, not only in their studies of the largest fright techniques, but also in the day-to-day trials of monsterdom. Despite their shortcomings — Ickis's insecurities, Oblina's bad temper, and Krumm's tendency to be a slacker — their friendship gets them through their hideous homework and horrendous adolescence. *Aaaahh! Real Monsters* is the second collaboration between Nickelodeon and Emmy and CableACE award-winning studio Klasky Csupo *(Rugrats).* Klasky Csupo's cutting-edge style of animation, paired with Nickelodeon's promise to deliver the unexpected to their kid audience, makes *Aaaahh! Real Monsters* a fantastic addition to the Nicktoons line-up.

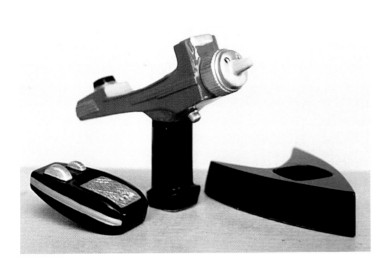

Row 1: *C-3PO and R2-D2* hand-painted bisque porcelain figurine, "C-3PO™ and R2-D2™ STAR WARS RETURN of the JEDI ©LUCASFILM LIMITED 1983 ALL RIGHTS RESERVED designed by sigma® the tastesetter™• MCMLXXXIII." On transparent label, "sigma© the tastesetter™ MADE IN TAIWAN." $25.00 – 35.00

C-3PO pencil tray, incised, "©LUCAS FILM LIMITED designed by sigma the tastesetter." Paper label, "sigma the tastesetter® PLEASE NOTE THAT ALL PIECES ARE HAND DECORATED SO COLOR VARIANCE COULD OCCUR, LABORATORY TESTED TO COMPLY WITH FDA GUIDELINES MADE IN JAPAN. $30.00 – 40.00

Row 2: *Luke Skywalker* hand-painted mug, "©LUCAS FILM LIMITED designed by sigma the tastesetter." Paper label, "sigma the tastesetter® PLEASE NOTE THAT ALL PIECES ARE HAND DECORATED SO COLOR VARIANCE COULD OCCUR, LABORATORY TESTED TO COMPLY WITH FDA GUIDELINES MADE IN JAPAN." $40.00 – 60.00

Gamorrean Guard hand-painted bisque porcelain figurine, "Gamorrean Guard™ STAR WARS RETURN of the JEDI ©LUCASFILM LIMITED 1983 ALL RIGHTS RESERVED designed by sigma® the tastesetter™• MCMLXXXIII." On transparent label, "sigma© the tastesetter™ MADE IN TAIWAN." $60.00 – 75.00

R2-D2 picture frame, on paper label, "Sigma the Tastesetter® PLEASE NOTE THAT ALL PIECES ARE HAND DECORATED SO COLOR VARIANCE COULD OCCUR, LABORATORY TESTED TO COMPLY WITH FDA GUIDELINES MADE IN JAPAN." $35.00 – 45.00

Row 3: *Darth Vader* telephone, "The Darth Vader™ Speaker Phone MODEL NO. DEIF 8040 PART NO. 205094-01 MFG. CODE 83 25 Complies with Part 68 F.C.C. Rules F.C.C. Registration Number: AA-499C-11316-MA-R Ringer Equivalence is 1.0B Made in Hong Kong" on paper label. "TM & © LUCASFILM LIMITED 1983, ALL RIGHTS RESERVED AMERICAN TELECOMMUNICATIONS CORP. AUTHORIZED USER." MIB $125.00 – 150.00

Below: *Darth Vader* ceramic bank by Roman Ceramics, "©1977 TWENTIETH CENTURY–FOX FILM CORPORATION STAR WARS ™ U.S.A." $150.00 – 175.00

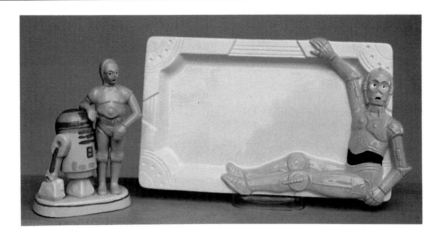

Row 1:   *Yoda* bank, "©LFL DESIGNED BY SIGMA THE TASTESETTER." Paper label, "sigma the tastesetter® PLEASE NOTE THAT ALL PIECES ARE HAND DECORATED SO COLOR VARIANCE COULD OCCUR, LABORATORY TESTED TO COMPLY WITH FDA GUIDELINES MADE IN JAPAN." $50.00 – 60.00

Yoda hand-painted mug, "©LUCAS FILM LIMITED designed by sigma the tastesetter." Paper label, "sigma the tastesetter® PLEASE NOTE THAT ALL PIECES ARE HAND DECORATED SO COLOR VARIANCE COULD OCCUR, LABORATORY TESTED TO COMPLY WITH FDA GUIDELINES MADE IN JAPAN." $25.00 – 35.00

Chewbacca hand-painted mug, "©LUCAS FILM LIMITED designed by sigma the tastesetter." Paper label, "sigma the tastesetter® PLEASE NOTE THAT ALL PIECES ARE HAND DECORATED SO COLOR VARIANCE COULD OCCUR, LABORATORY TESTED TO COMPLY WITH FDA GUIDELINES MADE IN JAPAN." $25.00 – 35.00

Chewbacca bank, "©LUCAS FILM LIMITED designed by sigma the tastesetter." Paper label, "Sigma the tastesetter® PLEASE NOTE THAT ALL PIECES ARE HAND DECORATED SO COLOR VARIANCE COULD OCCUR, LABORATORY TESTED TO COMPLY WITH FDA GUIDELINES MADE IN JAPAN." $50.00 – 60.00

Row 2:   *Wicket W. Warrick* hand-painted bisque porcelain figurine, "Wicket W. Warrick™ STAR WARS RETURN of the JEDI ©LUCASFILM LIMITED 1983 ALL RIGHTS RESERVED designed by sigma® the tastesetter™• MCMLXXXIII." On transparent label, "sigma© the tastesetter™ MADE IN TAIWAN." $25.00 – 35.00

Wicket W. Warrick face mug, "Wicket W. Warrick™ Star Wars RETURN OF THE JEDI© Lucas Film LTD 1983 All rights Reserved designed by Sigma® the Tastesetter™* ©MCMLXXXIII." $25.00 – 35.00

Klaatu hand-painted mug, "Klaatu™ STAR WARS RETURN OF THE JEDI™ ©LUCASFILM LIMITED 1983 ALL RIGHTS RESERVED designed by sigma® the tastesetter™ ©MCMLXXXIII." $25.00 – 35.00

Klaatu hand-painted bisque porcelain figurine, "Klaatu™ STAR WARS RETURN OF THE JEDI™ ©LUCASFILM LIMITED 1983 ALL RIGHTS RESERVED designed by sigma® the tastesetter™ ©MCMLXXXIII." On transparent label, "sigma© the tastesetter™ MADE IN TAIWAN." $25.00 – 35.00

Below: *Yoda* salt and pepper set, "DESIGNED BY SIGMA THE TASTESETTER © LFL." $200.00+

Row 1:   *Popeye* bank, "©1980 KING FEATURES SYNDICATE, INC.," Vandor. $90.00 – 100.00

Popeye covered box, incised, "©1990 KING FEATURES SYNDICATE, INC." Paper label, "Vandor® MADE IN JAPAN." $15.00 – 20.00

Popeye telephone, "© KFS INC. 1982." On bottom of base, "COM VU I MADE IN HONG KONG." On oval, gold, foil label, "PASSED O.C." $100.00 – 125.00

Row 2:   *Cathy* cookie jar, marked with fired-on decal, "CATHY KITCHEN COLLECTION CATHY © 1995 GUISEWITE STUDIO EXCLUSIVELY BY PAPEL®, ©FREELANCE, Made in Sri Lanka." 8½" high. $70.00 – 80.00

Mrs. Berenstain Bear, "THE BERENSTAIN BEARS™ © 1983 S&J Berenstain Made for Ebeling & Reuss Company." $575.00 – 625.00

Row 3:   *Graduating Bean* figurine, "ENESCO DESIGNED GIFTWARE SRI LANKA" on small, gold foil label. $12.00 – 15.00

Grandpa Bean figurine, "ENESCO DESIGNED GIFTWARE SRI LANKA" on small, gold foil label. $10.00 – 12.00

Bowling Bean bank, transparent paper label "HUMAN BEANS © 1981 Morgan Inc., Lic. Enesco Imports." Gold foil label, "ENESCO DESIGNED GIFTWARE SRI LANKA." $20.00 – 25.00

Nurse Bean, "ENESCO DESIGNED GIFTWARE SRI LANKA" on small, gold foil label. $12.00 – 15.00

Nurse Bean, transparent paper label, "HUMAN BEANS © 1981 Morgan Inc., Lic. Enesco Imports." Gold foil label, "ENESCO DESIGNED GIFTWARE SRI LANKA." $12.00 – 15.00

Below: *Christmas Bean* bank. $20.00 – 30.00

Row 1: *Betty's Kitchen* wall clock, "© 1995 VANDOR." Small, rectangular foil label "MADE IN TAIWAN." Triangular label, "VANDOR® KING FEATURES©." Second triangular label, "VANDOR® HAND PAINTED Brush strokes & color variations are a mark of unique quality." Discontinued. $45.00 – 55.00

Betty's utensil holder, "© 1995 VANDOR." Small, rectangular foil label "MADE IN TAIWAN." Triangular label, "VANDOR® KING FEATURES©." Second triangular label, "VANDOR® HAND PAINTED Brush strokes & color variations are a mark of unique quality." Discontinued.   Issue price $15.00

Row 2: *Betty's* covered sugar, "© 1995 VANDOR." Small, rectangular foil label "MADE IN TAIWAN." Triangular label, "VANDOR® KING FEATURES©." Second triangular label, "VANDOR® HAND PAINTED Brush strokes & color variations are a mark of unique quality."   Sugar/creamer set issue price $25.00

Betty's Kitchen teapot, "© 1995 VANDOR." Small, rectangular foil label "MADE IN TAIWAN." Triangular label, "VANDOR® KING FEATURES©." Second triangular label, "VANDOR® HAND PAINTED Brush strokes & color variations are a mark of unique quality."   Issue price $32.00

Betty's creamer, "© 1995 VANDOR." Small, rectangular foil label "MADE IN TAIWAN." Triangular label, "VANDOR® KING FEATURES©." Second triangular label, "VANDOR® HAND PAINTED Brush strokes & color variations are a mark of unique quality."   Creamer/sugar set issue price $25.00

Row 3: *Betty Boop Holiday* cookie jar, "VANDOR 1994." Round foil label, "MADE IN INDONESIA." There are two versions of this jar, one wearing a red bracelet and one wearing a yellow. The jar with the red bracelet is larger and older.   Issue price $50.00

Betty Boop Face bank, "1994 VANDOR." Small, rectangular foil label "MADE IN TAIWAN." Triangular label, "VANDOR® KING FEATURES©." Second triangular label, "VANDOR® HAND PAINTED Brush stokes & color variations are a mark of unique quality."   Issue price $14.00

Betty's Kitchen cookie jar, "© 1995 VANDOR." Small, rectangular foil label "MADE IN TAIWAN." Triangular label, "VANDOR® KING FEATURES©." Second triangular label, "VANDOR® HAND PAINTED Brush strokes & color variations are a mark of unique quality."   Issue price $50.00

Row 1: *Emmett Kelley* (Sr.), "EMMETT KELLY WORLD'S GREATEST CLOWN ©1983 Royal Manor ©Emmett Kelly Estate." $650.00 – 750.00

Uncle Mistletoe, unmarked, one of four known versions. Few may have any idea who the little guy with the top hat and bushy eyebrows is on top of Marshall Field's Christmas tree, but he was a pretty big dude in his day.

Created by Johanna Osborne at the request of her boss, Field's window display manager John Moss, Uncle Mistletoe, as he was called, first showed up in Field's Christmas windows in 1946. He was an immediate hit, becoming the store's Christmas symbol. By 1948 he had his own TV show and daily drew crowds of 250,000 fans, who visited him and his wife, Aunt Holly, in Cloud Cottage on the store's eighth floor. $1,000.00+

Row 2: *Bonzo,* "COPYRIGHT 1951." The owners of this jar (Jerry and Lona Spier) believe this character was taken from the movie, *Bedtime For Bonzo,* starring Ronald Reagan. Spier. Price not determined.

Alice in Wonderland, unmarked, of unknown origin. This "prototype" was originally all white, cold paint was added for accent. Price not determined.

Below: *Star Trek Enterprise* stoneware cylinder, "PFALTZGRAFF STAR TREK®™, ® and © 1993 Par. Pic. All rights reserved." Produced in 1993 by Pfaltzgraff of York, PA, as a gift item to accompany their 3-piece stoneware buffet set. $35.00 – 45.00

Row 1: *Norfin Troll,* International Silver Company logo and "INTERNATIONAL SILVER COMPANY" incised into bottom of base (two lines). Paper label, "© The Troll Co., APS 1992 NORFIN® is a reg. TM of EFS Mkg. Made in Taiwan" (three lines). Another paper label with, "WARNING NOT DISHWASHER SAFE" (two lines). $60.00 – 75.00

Norfin Troll bank, paper label, "INTERNATIONAL SILVER COMPANY" incised into bottom of base (two lines). "©The Troll Co., APS 1992, NORFIN® is a reg. TM of EFS Mkg., Made in Taiwan." Second paper label, "WARNING, NOT DISHWASHER SAFE." $25.00 – 35.00

Row 2: *Ziggy* telephone, "ZIGGY® by Tom Wilson, © 1990 ZIGGY & FRIENDS, INC., MANUFACTURED BY TYCO INDUSTRIES, INC., MOORESTOWN, N.J. 08057, MADE IN CHINA." Inside receiver, "TYCO INDUSTRIES, INC. MODEL 1268, COMPLIES WITH PART 68 FCC RULES, FCC NO. IPSCHN-18294-TE-E REN: 0.5A, USOC: RJ11C MADE IN CHINA." $60.00 – 80.00

Ziggy bank, "Designer Collection by Tom Wilson Earthenware Ziggy™©MCMLXXXII WWA INC WWA INC CLEVELAND USA 44144 MADE IN KOREA." $35.00 – 50.00

Ziggy PVC bank, unmarked. $30.00 – 45.00

Row 3: *Ziggy* cylinder by Marsh, 9½" high, "Ziggy™ by Tom Wilson ©1985 Universal Press Syndicate." Candee. $70.00 – 90.00

Teddy Bear cylinder, 10½" high, "© Bialosky & Friends 1983." Candee. $70.00 – 90.00

Below: *Chilly Willy,* "A3391/CW." Honchar. $900.00 – 1,100.00

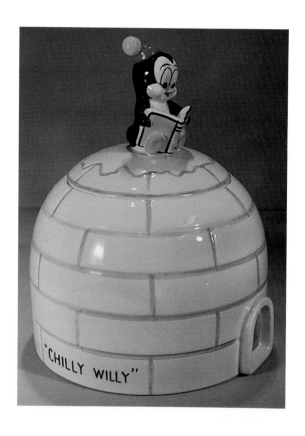

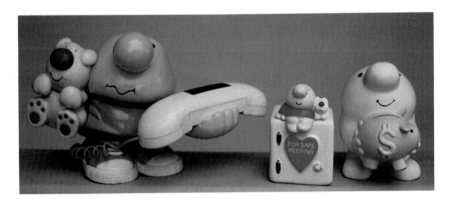

Row 1: *Garfield* piggy bank, 7¾" high, "©PAWS." Issue price $19.99

Row 2: *Garfield* wall-hanging telephone. $40.00 – 50.00

Garfield bank, "GARFIELD: ©1978, 1981 United Feature syndicate, Inc. Licensee Enesco Corporation Made In China." $25.00 – 35.00

Garfield telephone. $25.00 – 35.00

Row 3: *Socks™ The White House Cat™,* reusable, plastic cat food container, "Manufactured and distributed by STREET KIDS CORP., CA 90230 © 1993 STREET KIDS CORP. ALL RIGHTS RESERVED." $4.00 – 6.00

Socks™, The White House Cat™ cookie jar. $35.00 – 45.00

Below: *Pink Panther* "GALLERY COLLECTION PINK PANTHER by Treasure Craft Limited Edition #775 of 1000 pieces. Made in Mexico ©1995 UAP." Price with certificate of authenticity: $175.00 – 200.00

Pink Panther face mask by Royal Orleans, stamped "Pink Panther Collection exclusively destributed by Royal Orleans ™ and © 1981 United Artists. All rights reserved." Armstrong. $70.00 – 90.00

Pink Panther salt and pepper set by Royal Orleans, 3½" high, "©1982 U. A." Armstrong. $225.00+

Pink Panther picture frame by Royal Orleans, Armstrong. "©UAC Geoffrey." $50.00 – 60.00

CHRISTMAS

Row 1: *True Meaning of Christmas* cookie jar, modeled for Fred and Joyce Roerig *(Cookie Jarrin')* by Don Winton. Christmas has always been very special to Joyce. As Herndon Joseph, the Roerig grandson, grew, it became apparent how important it was to teach little ones the true meaning of Christmas.

Issue price $149.00

Row 2: *The Night Before Christmas* jar was introduced for Christmas 1995, and available exclusively through The Franklin Mint. Each jar came with a certificate of authenticity telling this story within the center fold: *"Christmas is a holiday that many different cultures celebrate in a variety of ways. One common ingredient among all the various Christmas customs, however, is the Christmas feast. And while the types of food offered vary from country to country, sharing a meal with one's loved ones at Christmas time is a unifying custom around the globe.*

The Christmas feast may be traced back to the traditional winter feast when farmers would kill their livestock because of dwindling fodder supplies. With the arrival of Christianity in Europe, the winter feast became associated with the Christmas season. At first oxen were used, then pigs, and later boars. Indeed, the boar became such a familiar Christmas meat that in Scandinavia, bread shaped into the figure of a boar was eaten at Christmas.

Fowl also played an important role at the Christmas table. In England, peacocks were roasted and then dressed again in their brilliant feathers, and in Germany, the goose was adopted as the Christmas dish — a custom that continues in popularity throughout Europe. In America, the turkey was a favorite bird, and its use at the Christmas table has spread throughout the world.

Besides these hearty dishes, Christmas is also noted for the many flavorful and uniquely decorated cakes and cookies that mark the season. So popular were these sweet treats — and baked in such fascinating shapes — that often they were also used as ornaments. Cookies and cakes also play an important part in other Christmas rituals, such as special treats left by excited children for the expected arrival of Santa Claus with his sleigh full of gifts.

Now the spirit and joy of Christmas is celebrated in a marvelous work of art by renowned artist Jonathan Goode. The Night Before Christmas Cookie Jar is crafted in fine porcelain, hand-painted in brilliant colors and decorated with shimmering accents of 24 karat gold and is a delightful addition to your holiday decor."

Impressively, marked with a circular decal of fired gold, "THE NIGHT BEFORE CHRISTMAS COOKIE JAR • FINE PORCELAIN • THE FRANKLIN MINT."

Issue price $135.00

Row 1: *Theodore Bear's Christmas,* Tienshan®, "Do Not Put In Dishwasher, Use a Soft Damp Cloth Or Soft Sponge To Clean. NOT INTENDED TO HOLD LIQUID, MADE IN CHINA." $25.00 – 35.00

Goose, distributed by Roses's Stores Inc. Henderson, NC 27536, "MADE IN CHINA" on small, gold-colored, rectangular paper label. $20.00 – 30.00

Row 2: *Jolly Santa,* Home for the Holidays Collection, "© MCE, EDI SAUSALITO, CA. MADE IN CHINA." Paper label "NOT INTENDED FOR USE IN MICROWAVE OR CONVENTIONAL OVENS RECOMMEND HAND WASH WARM WATER." $25.00 – 35.00

Windsor Collection Santa, paper label "HAND WASH ONLY WITH SPONGE. DO NOT SCRUB. DO NOT PUT IN DISHWASHER." Small, gold-colored rectangular label "MADE IN TAIWAN." $30.00 – 40.00

Row 3: *Santa Calls,* the leading character from the book, *Santa Calls* by William Joyce. Stamped on the flat, unglazed bottom of the base "SAKS FIFTH AVENUE NO.___, EDITION 3000, CHRISTMAS 1995." $150.00 – 175.00

Santa Calls, the leading character from the book, *Santa Calls* by William Joyce. Stamped on the flat, unglazed bottom of the base is the signature of William Joyce and "SAKS FIFTH AVENUE NO.___, EDITION 3000, CHRISTMAS 1994." In reality, there were closer to 1,000 than the 3,000 stated on the jar. The Santa Calls jars, produced by Treasure Craft for Saks Fifth Avenue, are at the top of Joyce's favorite list of Christmas cookie jars. Though the 1994 version seems to be favored among collectors, in our eyes they are equal. $150.00 – 175.00

Below: *Santa,* HomeTrends™, "ASIA MASTER GROUP INCORPORATED IN HONG KONG MADE IN CHINA." Marketed by Wal-Mart Stores, Inc. Bentonville, Arkansas 72716. $20.00 – 25.00

Holiday Bear, ©1993 (GHA) Grant-Howard Assoc., Norwalk, CT 06854, musical, plays *Jingle Bells.* Incised "© H CARTWRIGHT." Small, oval, gold-colored paper label "MADE IN CHINA." $25.00 – 35.00

Musical Santa, ©1993 (GHA) Grant-Howard Assoc., Norwalk, CT 06844, plays *Santa Claus is Coming to Town* and *Rudolph.* Small, oval, gold-colored paper label "MADE IN CHINA." $25.00 – 35.00

Row 1:   *Snowman with Broom,* stamped "COOKS CLUB INC Harrison NJ 07029.
Made in China." Paper label "THIS BAG IS NOT A TOY *WARNING* TO
AVOID DANGER OF SUFFOCATION KEEP THIS BAG AWAY FROM BABIES AND
CHILDREN. DO NOT USE IN CRIBS, BEDS, CARRIAGES OR PLAY PENS.
THIS BAG IS NOT A TOY: TEAR UP BAG BEFORE THROWING AWAY." $25.00 – 35.00

Snowman Decorating Tree, stamped "WORLD BAZAARS INC." On small,
oval gold-colored label, "MADE IN CHINA." $25.00 – 35.00

Snowman (broom and redbird), World Bazaars, Inc., "DELICATE HAND-PAINTED
SURFACE • HAND WASH ONLY WITH SPONGE • USE A DAMP CLOTH TO
CLEAN • DO NOT USE BRUSH OR SCRUB • DO NOT PUT IN DISHWASHER."
On small, oval gold-colored label, "MADE IN CHINA." $25.00 – 35.00

Row 2:   *Santa and Rudolph,* "à la carte J C Penney styles for the home. Made in
China. Hand wash only. Not recommended for use in a Microwave
Oven."   Issue price $24.99

Santa with Toy Pack, "à la carte J C Penney styles for the home. Made in
China. Hand wash only. Not recommended for use in a Microwave
Oven."   Issue price $24.99

Santa and Elf, "à la carte J C Penney styles for the home. Made in
China. Hand wash only. Not recommended for use in a Microwave
Oven."   Issue price $24.99

Row 3:   *Reindeer in Sweater,* May Department Stores, incised "MADE IN
CHINA." Stamped "Celebrate the Season." $25.00 – 35.00

Trevor Bear, 1994 Hallmark, embossed "NOT DISHWASHER SAFE."
On small, oval gold-colored label "MADE IN CHINA." introduced
in 1995 at Hallmark. $25.00 – 35.00

Reindeer in Santa hat/sweater, stamped "Holly Tree™ MADE IN
CHINA." Incised "MADE IN CHINA." $25.00 – 35.00

Row 1: *Santa Head* small canister, "The Cook's Bazaar." On paper label "Made in Taiwan."   Set $30.00 – 40.00

Santa Head large canister, "The Cook's Bazaar." On paper label "Made in Taiwan."   Set $30.00 – 40.00

Santa Head medium canister, "The Cook's Bazaar." On paper label "Made in Taiwan."   Set $30.00 – 40.00

Row 2: *Bear in Cookie Jar*, paper label on bottom "Made in Japan." Stamped under glaze "Dayton's 1987." $25.00 – 35.00

Santa in chimney, unmarked. $25.00 – 35.00

Sleigh with Toys, paper label "Made in Taiwan." $25.00 – 35.00

Row 3: *Snowman*, paper label "Made in China." $25.00 – 35.00

Toy Soldier, "The Cook's Bizarre, Made in Taiwan." $25.00 – 35.00

Snowman, unmarked. $25.00 – 35.00

Below: *Snowman*, "© O'Well Novelty 1994, Made in China." $25.00 – 35.00

Rocking Horse, "© O'Well Novelty 1994, Made in China." $25.00 – 35.00

Row 1:   *Teddy Bear* wearing Santa Bear slippers. Marked with small oval
gold foil label "MADE IN CHINA."   Issue price $19.95

Santa with gnarled wood staff. On box "Holiday Home by Home Accents
Ceramic Christmas Cookie Jar Made in China Manufactured For Belk Stores
Service, Inc. S/3603." Marked with gold foil label
"MADE IN CHINA."   Issue price $24.99

Santa Head/holly finial, info on box "Holiday Home by Home
Accents Made in China. Manufactured for Belk Stores Services,
Inc. S/3600." Jar unmarked.   Issue price $24.99

Row 2:   *Santa* decorating tree with cat and dog. Marked with green back stamp
"HOME FOR THE HOLIDAYS, MADE IN CHINA." $30.00 – 40.00

Bear, © 1996 May Department Store Company. Marked on bottom of jar with
green back stamp "Celebrate the Season."   Issue price $30.00

Stocking by May Department Stores Company 1996. Marked with
impressed "MADE IN CHINA." Green back stamp "Celebrate the
Season."   Issue price $38.00

Row 3:   *Gingerbread Man.* Impressed "©1996 JAY IMPORT CO INC, MADE IN CHINA."
Box marked "Marketed by Wal-Mart Stores, Inc. Bentonville, AR 72716."   Issue price $10.97

Old World Santa. Impressed "ROSEGARDEN, MADE IN CHINA." Box marked
"HOMETRENDS, Marketed by Wal-Mart Stores, Inc. Bentonville,
AR 72716."   Issue price $10.97

Christmas Fireplace. Embossed on bottom "©LR1966." Box "Marketed by
Wal-Mart Stores, Inc. Bentonville, AR 72716 Made in China."   Issue price $10.97

Below: *Santa Cowhand,* musical, plays *Jingle Bells* when lid is lifted. Stamped
under glaze, "ASIA MASTER." Small, oval, gold-colored label "MADE IN
CHINA." Distributed by Pamida Stores, Inc., Omaha, NE. $23.00 – 28.00

Snowman (Collins Creative Kitchen) with bag of candy distributed by
Ben Franklin Stores, Inc. Carol Stream, Illinois 60188." Marked only with
small, gold-colored, rectangular paper label "MADE IN CHINA." $18.00 – 22.00

Santa Gnome, distributed by Pamida Stores, Inc., Omaha, NE. "MADE IN
CHINA" stamped on small, oval, gold-colored label. $18.00 – 22.00

CLAY ART

Michael Zanfagna and Jenny McLain began Clay Art in the back room of a living space in 1979. Their first product was the Cherub's Fanny Hook; they gained attention with the introduction of their ceramic masks of Hollywood stars. The first cookie jar from Clay Art was Catfish in 1989. Matching cookie plates for five of the jars were introduced in 1995 and ethnic jars were brought out in 1996. All items are hand painted and the line currently includes masks, mugs, shakers, and table top items, many of which coordinate, as well as papier mache accessories and wooden utensils. Clay Art items are available retail around the US.

Row 1: *Catfish* salt or pepper shaker (large), stamped, "© 1992 CLAY ART San Francisco, MADE IN PHILIPPINES." Snyder.   Set $18.00 – 22.00

Catfish cookie jar, "CLAY ART 'CATFISH SERIES' ©1990 CLAY ART MADE IN PHILIPPINES." $35.00 – 45.00

Catfish salt or pepper shaker (large), stamped, "© 1992 CLAY ART San Francisco, MADE IN PHILIPPINES." Snyder.   Set $18.00 – 22.00

Mama Cat, "CLAY ART 'Mama Cat' © 1992 CLAY ART SAN FRANCISCO, MADE IN TAIWAN." $35.00 – 45.00

Catfish salt or pepper shaker (small), "CLAY ART, MADE IN PHILIPPINES" on paper label.   Set $18.00 – 22.00

Catfish cookie jar, "CLAY ART 'CATFISH SERIES' © 1990 CLAY ART MADE IN PHILIPPINES." $35.00 – 45.00

Catfish salt or pepper shaker (small), "CLAY ART, MADE IN PHILIPPINES" on paper label.   Set $18.00 – 22.00

Row 2: *Humpty Dumpty,* "CLAY ART HUMPTY DUMPTY SERIES © 1991 CLAY ART." $100.00 – 125.00

Catnap cookie jar, stamped "CLAY ART 'CATNIP SERIES' © 1991 CLAY ART SAN FRANCISCO, MADE IN PHILIPPINES." $35.00 – 45.00

Catnap salt and pepper set, "CLAY ART MADE IN THE PHILIPPINES" on paper label.   Set $18.00 – 22.00

Dogbone cookie jar, stamped, "CLAY ART 'DOG BONE' SERIES ©1991 CLAY ART." Paper label, "MADE IN TAIWAN." $35.00 – 45.00

Row 3: *Cabbage Bunny* cookie jar, "CLAY ART 'CABBAGE BUNNY' © 1992 CLAY ART SAN FRANCISCO MADE IN TAIWAN." $35.00 – 45.00

Teddy Bear, stamped, "CLAY ART TEDDY BEAR SERIES © 1991 CLAY ART • MADE IN TAIWAN." $35.00 – 45.00

Sunday Cow, "CLAY ART SUNDAY BEST COW © 1992 CLAY ART SAN FRANCISCO." Stamped, "MADE IN TAIWAN." On paper label, "HAND PAINTED © CLAY ART." $35.00 – 45.00

Row 1: *Pig Watermelon,* 8½" high, "CLAY ART HAND PAINTED PIG WATERMELON
SAN FRANCISCO MADE IN TAIWAN." $35.00 – 45.00

Barnyard Santa, "CLAY ART HAND PAINTED BARNYARD SANTA © CLAY
ART 1993 San Francisco MADE IN TAIWAN." $35.00 – 45.00

Row 2: *Stacked Animals,* stamped under glaze "Stacked Animals series © 1991
CLAY ART MADE IN PHILIPPINES." $35.00 – 45.00

Pig Out salt and pepper set, paper label "CLAY ART MADE IN THE
PHILIPPINES." Set $18.00 – 22.00

Pig Out cookie jar, "Hand painted © Clay Art" on paper label. Stamped
under glaze "CLAY ART Pig Out series © 1991 CLAY ART MADE IN
PHILIPPINES." $35.00 – 45.00

Row 3: *Wizard of Oz* cookie jar, "Hand painted © CLAY ART" on paper label.
Stamped under glaze "WIZARD of OZ © 1939 LOEW'S Inc., Ren.,
MGM 1966 © 1990 TURNER ENTERTAINMENT CO., ALL RIGHTS
RESERVED © 1990." $125.00 – 150.00

Merlin and Dragon teapot, stamped under glaze "CLAY ART ENCHANTMENT
SERIES © 1990 CLAY ART SAN FRANCISCO MADE IN PHILIPPINES." $70.00 – 80.00

Merlin and Dragon salt and pepper set. Set $35.00 – 45.00

Midnight Snack cookie jar, "Hand painted © Clay Art" on paper label.
Stamped under glaze "CLAY ART HOME SWEET HOME SERIES © 1991
CLAY ART MADE IN PHILIPPINES." $50.00 – 60.00

Below: *Road Hog,* "CLAY ART SAN FRANCISCO COOKIE JAR, ROAD HOG
©1995 CLAY ART, HAND PAINTED, MADE IN CHINA." Incised into
bottom of base "C.A." Issue price $50.00

Cow Racer, "CLAY ART COOKIE JAR COW RACER © 1994 CLAY ART
HAND PAINTED SAN FRANCISCO MADE IN TAIWAN." $40.00 – 50.00

DeFOREST OF CALIFORNIA

Row 1: *Cocky and Henny* (DeForest Dandees) salt and pepper set, unmarked. Darrow. $40.00 – 60.00

Henny (Dandee Hen) cookie jar, "DeForest of Calif. USA." Darrow. $200.00 – 225.00

Cocky (Dandee Rooster) cookie jar, "DeForest of California Hand Painted." Darrow. $325.00 – 350.00

Row 2: *Henny* (DeForest Dandees) dip and chip, 11" tray, "DeForest of California © 1956." Henny (center), 5" high. Available in green, charcoal, brown. Darrow. $60.00 – 70.00

Henny lazy susan, 14", available in green, charcoal, brown. Turntable, "DeForest of California © 1958 USA." Henny (center), "DeForest of California Hand Painted." Darrow. $150.00 – 175.00

Row 3: *Bar-B-Cutie* salad plate, 6", "DeForest of California, hand painted." Darrow. $18.00 – 22.00

Bar-B-Cutie salad plate, 6", "DeForest of California, hand painted." Darrow. $18.00 – 22.00

Bar-B-Cutie dinner plate, 11", "DeForest of California, hand painted." Darrow. $25.00 – 30.00

Bar-B-Cutie chop plate, 15", "DeForest of California, hand painted." Darrow. $35.00 – 45.00

Row 4: *Bar-B-Cutie* salt and pepper set, unmarked. Potter. $30.00 – 40.00

Bar-B-Cutie salt and pepper set, unmarked. Potter. $30.00 – 40.00

Bar-B-Cutie tureen with ladle. Tureen, 12" x 8". "DeForest of California, hand painted." Potter. $175.00 – 195.00

Additional items available in Bar-B-Cutie: 6" sauce dish, 13" x 2½" salad bowl, 8" x 11" divided relish, 10 oz. cup and saucer, 8" high oil and vinegar, 5" high cream and sugar, and 6" soup bowl.

Row 1: *Pig,* "DeForest of California © 1956." Darrow. $100.00 – 125.00

Goody Bank, Goody's head is a bank, "DeForest of California © 1956." Available in brown or pink. Darrow. $225.00 – 275.00

Goody bank, Goody's head is a bank, "DeForest of California © 1956." Available in brown or pink. Darrow. $225.00 – 275.00

Peter Porker, "DeForest of Calif. © 1956." Darrow. $225.00 – 275.00

Row 2: *Pig Head,* unmarked. Darrow. $50.00 – 55.00

Perky, 7" high, "De Forest of California Hand Painted." Darrow. $55.00 – 65.00

Perky, 7" high, "De Forest of California Hand Painted." Darrow. $55.00 – 65.00

Perky, 2-qt. pitcher in brown or pink. There is a matching 16oz. mug (not shown). Darrow. $65.00 – 75.00

Row 3: *Pig* hors de'oeuvre, unmarked. Darrow. $10.00 – 15.00

Dippy Pig dip set from the Peter Porker Line. Eleven inch tray with Dippy resting in the center, "DeForest of California © 1956." Available in brown or pink. Darrow. $75.00 – 95.00

Hamburger relish condiment, "DeForest of California © 1956." Darrow. $25.00 – 30.00

Row 4: *Beans,* "DeForest of California 19©59." Darrow. $100.00 – 125.00

Candy, "DeForest of California 19©59." Darrow. $50.00 – 65.00

Chubby, 3" high, for relish and mustard. Colors: brown or pink, "DeForest of California Hand painted." Darrow. $35.00 – 45.00

Below: *Perky,* Lazy Susan, 14" in brown or pink. Darrow. $200.00 – 225.00

Hammy Jr., divided relish, 9" x 10", in pink or brown, "© 11-15-1957 DeForest of Calif. USA." Potter. $55.00 – 65.00

Rolling pin, "DeForest of California." Potter. $75.00 – 85.00

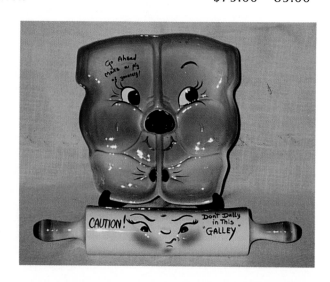

Row 1:   *Cheese* salt shaker, unmarked. Potter. $25.00 – 30.00

                Cheezy condiment, "DeForest of California Hand Painted." Potter. $25.00 – 30.00

                Big Cheese condiment, "DeForest of California Hand Painted." Potter. $40.00 – 50.00

                Cheese pepper shaker, unmarked. Potter. $25.00 – 30.00

Row 2:   *Pig* (pink glaze) creamer, "DeForest of California © 1956." Potter. $30.00 – 40.00

                Pig Head cookie jar, "DeForest of California Hand Painted." Potter. $70.00 – 90.00

                Pig (brown glaze) creamer, "DeForest of California Hand Painted."
Potter. $25.00 – 35.00

Row 3:   *Peppy* pepper shaker, part of Perky's 3-piece range set, unmarked.
Potter.   3-piece set $100.00 – 125.00

                Drippin's, part of Perky's 3-piece range set, unmarked.
Potter.   3-piece set $100.00 – 125.00

                Salty salt shaker, part of Perky's 3-piece range set, unmarked.
Potter.   3-piece set $100.00 – 125.00

Below: *Hammy* platter, DeForest 19©56." $60.00 – 70.00

                Tea Set stackable teapot, creamer, and sugar, "DeForest of
California." Darrow. $60.00 – 70.00

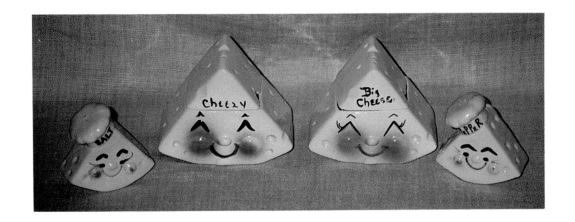

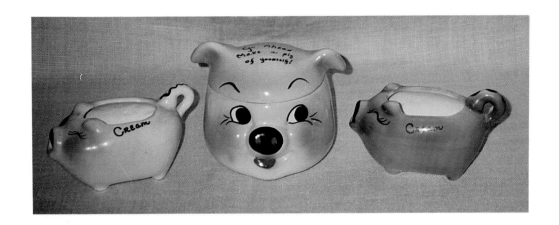

Row 1:   *Peanut* (squirrel finial) covered container, "DeForest of California
Hand Painted." $25.00 – 35.00

Spooners double spoon rest, "DeForest of California Hand Painted." $75.00 – 95.00

Lil Angel, "DeForest of California © 1957," billed as "the perfect girlfriend
for the Holy Devil AKA Halo Boy" (see *Book I,* page 232). $725.00 – 775.00

Row 2:   *Clown,* "DeForest of CA U.S.A." on sides of shoes in back, not on
bottom of jar. Potter. $125.00 – 175.00

King, "DeForest of California © 1957." Potter. $800.00+

Row 3:   *Onion* condiment, "DeForest of California Hand Painted." Potter. $25.00 – 35.00

Onion condiment, "DeForest of California Hand Painted." Potter. $25.00 – 35.00

Onion condiment, "DeForest of California Hand Painted." Potter. $25.00 – 35.00

Horace Radish condiment, "DeForest of California Hand
Painted." Potter. $55.00 – 65.00

Below: De Forest of California, Inc. catalog sheet
5502 *Klown.* $45.00 – 55.00
5537 *Owl.* $30.00 – 35.00
5516 *Monkey.* $45.00 – 55.00
5538 *Barrel.* $20.00 – 30.00
5506 *Elephant.* $35.00 – 45.00
5523 *Ranger Bear.* $35.00 – 45.00

138

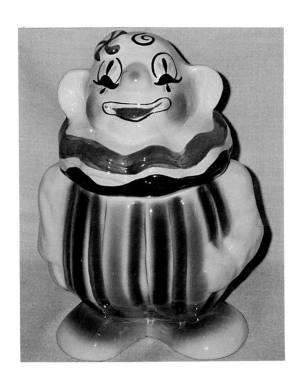

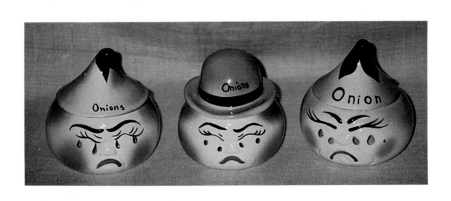

Row 1:   *Poodle,* "19©60 DeForest of California USA." Darrow. $40.00 – 50.00

          Barrel, "DeForest of California 553." $20.00 – 30.00

          Floral, elephant finial, "DeForest of Calif. USA 530." $40.00 – 50.00

Row 2:   *Gem,* "DeForest of California Hand Painted." Darrow. $40.00 – 50.00

          Gem, unmarked. Darrow. $30.00 – 40.00

Below: DeForest of California, Inc. catalog sheet:
          5515 *Puppy.* $45.00 – 55.00
          5524 *Lamb.* $40.00 – 50.00
          5522 *Padre.* $75.00 – 95.00
          5526 *Bunny.* $40.00 – 50.00
          5514 *Chipmunk.* $45.00 – 55.00

DEPARTMENT 56 INC.

Additional items distributed by Dept. 56, the Eden Prairie, Minnesota, importer/distributor, are featured in Book II.

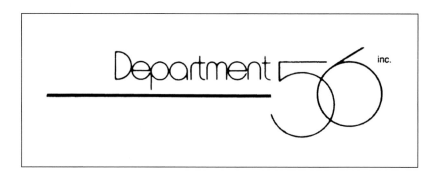

Row 1: *Peasant Woman,* "Dept. 56 Peasant people © 1980" incised and on paper label. Potter. $100.00 – 125.00

Cowboy in silhouette salt or pepper shaker, "Dept. 56." This jar is reversible, red on one side, yellow on the other. Candee. $25.00 – 30.00

Cowboy in silhouette, 10½" high, "Dept. 56." This jar is reversible, red on one side, yellow on the other. Candee. $90.00 – 110.00

Row 2: *Vegetable Cottage,* incised, "©Department 56 1001." Paper label, "© Dept 56 Inc. Made in Taiwan R.O.C." Honchar. $50.00 – 60.00

Vegetable House, incised, "©Department 56 1990." Paper label, "©Dept 56 Inc. Made in Taiwan R.O.C." Honchar. $60.00 – 75.00

DORANNE OF CALIFORNIA
1951 – 1991

See *Books I* and *II* for additional, extensive coverage of Doranne cookie jars.

Row 1:   *Jack Rabbit,* 13" high. Slyce. $40.00 – 50.00

Hen trivet, "DORANNE OF CALIFORNIA TV-30." $18.00 – 22.00

Donkey (red tie), "CJ - 108." $50.00 – 60.00

Row 2:   *Doctor,* "CJ-130 © U.S.A., DORANNE CA." $225.00- – 275.00

School Bus, "DORANNE California CJ 120 © USA." $150.00 – 175.00

Row 3:   *Bear Essentials,* "Doranne Calif., BE-19 ©." $50.00 – 60.00

Opossum, unmarked. $40.00 – 50.00

Below: *Cow on Moon,* "J 2 USA." Darrow. $350.00 – 375.00

Elephant, "DORANNE OF CALIF. CJ144." $50.00 – 60.00

ENESCO

Enesco is an Elk Grove, Illinois, based importer/distributor.

Row 1: *Mother-in-the-Kitchen* toothpick holder, "Imports Enesco Japan." Horelica. .... $18.00 – 22.00

Mother-in-the-Kitchen salt or pepper shaker, "Imports, Enesco Japan." Horelica. .... $25.00 – 30.00

Mother-in-the-Kitchen cookie jar, 9½" tall, paper label "Imports, Enesco Japan." Horelica. .... $250.00 – 275.00

Mother-in-the-Kitchen salt or pepper shaker, "Imports, Enesco Japan." Horelica. .... $25.00 – 30.00

Row 2: *Mother-in-the-Kitchen* salt or pepper shaker, "Imports, Enesco Japan." Horelica. .... $22.00 – 25.00

Mother-in-the-Kitchen cookie jar, 9½" tall, "Imports Enesco Japan." Horelica. .... $225.00 – 250.00

Mother-in-the-Kitchen salt or pepper shaker, "Imports, Enesco, Japan." .... $22.00 – 25.00

Below: *Bear Pull-toy,* "The Enesco Artists' Gallery PRESENTS COME AND JOIN THE TEDDY BEAR PARADE © 1996 Enesco Corporation. Designed by Claudia Stenvig-Olsen 269360 MADE IN CHINA." Incised into bottom "*Claudia Stenvig Olsen.*" .... Issue price $60.00

Row 1: *Bear,* Signature Store exclusive, "The Enesco Precious Moments Collection, ©1993 Samuel J. Butcher, All rights reserved worldwide, Licensee Enesco Corporation, Made in China." $75.00 – 95.00

Frosty the Snowman, "Frosty Snowman™ Frosty the Snowman, Characters, Names and All Related Indicia Are Trademarks of Warner/Chappell Music, Inc. ©1994 LICENSEE ENESCO CORPORATION Made in Taiwan ROC." $50.00 – 60.00

Mary's Moo Moo, here a moo, there a moo, "©1993 ENESCO CORPORATION DESIGNED BY MARY RHYNER MADE IN TAIWAN." $40.00 – 50.00

Row 2: *Lucy 'n Me Bear,* by Lucy King, distributed by Enesco. Armstrong. $125.00 – 150.00

Owl, 8¼" high, "E-9227 ©1997 ENESCO." Boone. $20.00 – 30.00

Bulldog, distributed by Enesco. $50.00 – 60.00

Row 3: *Dear God Kids* (girl) bank, "©1982 INTERCONTINENTAL LICENSEE ENESCO." Paper label "ENESCO MADE IN TAIWAN." $40.00 – 50.00

Dear God Kids (boy) candy container, "©1983 INTERCONTINENTAL LICENSEE ENESCO." $70.00 – 80.00

Dear God Kids (girl) candy container, "©1983 INTERCONTINENTAL LICENSEE ENESCO." $70.00 – 80.00

Below: *Clown Head,* "Enesco Imports Japan E-5835." Blumenfeld. $125.00 – 150.00

GOEBEL

Hummelwerk Porcelain Manufactory was founded by F. W. Goebel in Rodental, West Germany, in 1871. Sculpted in 1983 by Gerhard Wittman, the Goebel head jars were produced only in 1983 for North America, and distributed by Goebel US (Hummelwerk Elmsford at that time). Suggested retail prices in 1983 were $38.00 each. All carry the same mark, "Goebel W. Germany" (2 lines), on the bottom of base.

Row 1: *Lion,* "Goebel W. Germany." Honchar. $70.00 – 80.00

Row 2: *Panda Bear,* "Goebel W. Germany." Honchar. $70.00 – 80.00

Owl, "Goebel W. Germany." Honchar. $70.00 – 80.00

Parrot, "Goebel W. Germany." Honchar. $70.00 – 80.00

Row 3: *Pig,* "Goebel W. Germany." Honchar. $100.00 – 125.00

Dog, "Goebel W. Germany." Honchar. $100.00 – 125.00

Cat, "Goebel W. Germany." Honchar. $100.00 – 125.00

The old Cardinal also came in a trademark 3, which is similar to Trademark 4.

Below: *Friar Tuck,* "K 29 Made in W. Germany 1957." $375.00 – 475.00

Cardinal, "K 29 © by W. Goebel W. Germany © 1957." Trademark 4 also has a V with a stylized bee embossed onto the bottom of the jar. Wuttke. $1,750.00 – 2,000.00

The K 29 (Friar) cookie jar or biscuit barrel can be found with every trademark from full bee to TMK 6. There are two variations of the Friar, one matte (TMK 2-5), and one glossy with a black collar (TMK 5-6).

The first cookie jars produced have the full bee. Some, with early stylized trademarks also have a 1956 copyright date. All later trademark jars have a 1957 date. The only mold difference is the date.

The black collar cookie jar was made in very limited quantities and usually brings a small premium over solid brown.

The old Cardinal (TMK 3-4) is by far the hardest to find.

HALLMARK CARDS, INC.

Hallmark Cards, Inc., of Kansas City, Missouri, is a major contributing factor in the collectible field, though most associate this name with ornaments.

Not all of Mary Engelbreit's works are exclusive to Hallmark; Maxine on the other hand is Hallmark through and through.

Row 1:   *Friendship Garden* by Mary Engelbreit. On bottom of base
"Friendship is the Sweetest treat of all. Hallmark GALLERIES
   "Mary Engelbreit's Friendship Garden number: _____of 9,500 ©
1993 Mary Engelbreit, Hallmark Cards, Inc. QHG5009, Made in Thailand."
   A note with a special message from Mary Engelbreit is included
with each jar. "My work has always been very personal. Many of my
drawings are based on events and people in my own life. Friendship
is one of my favorite themes, and in these Hallmark Galleries pieces
I celebrate the joys of friendship through images rendered in bright,
cheerful colors. I hope that the happiness I felt when creating these
designs will be shared by those who view them." $70.00 – 80.00

Row 2:   *Maxine, "J Wagner © Hallmark Cards, Inc."*   Issue price $24.95

HAPPY MEMORIES

Bill and Loretta Hamburg founded Happy Memories Collectibles in 1986, buying and selling collectible toys and cookie jars. In 1993 they designed and introduced a line of limited edition bronze sculptures based on famous movie and television cowboys. In 1994 they brought out their Hollywood Legends series of limited edition cookie jars beginning with Hopalong Cassidy with Topper, and then James Dean. Marilyn Monroe, Elvis Presley, and Scarlett O'Hara have been added since. The company produces their jars in small numbers; each is fully authorized and licensed by the trademark owners.

Row 1:   *Elvis Presley,* 14¾" high, 11½" wide, "HAPPY MEMORIES COLLECTIBLES
Woodland Hills, California. ELVIS™ LIMITED EDITION #____ of 1250.
Elvis and Elvis Presley are registered trademarks of Elvis Presley
Enterprises, Inc. © 1997 Elvis Presley Enterprises, Inc." There is also
a hologram on the bottom that states: "E.P.E. OFFICIAL PRODUCT." $280.00 – 300.00

Scarlett O'Hara, 13¼" high, 10" wide, "HAPPY MEMORIES COLLECTIBLES
Woodland Hills, California. SCARLETT O'HARA™ LIMITED EDITION
#____ of 500 ©1996 TURNER ENTERTAINMENT CO. ALL RIGHTS RESERVED.
Gone With the Wind™, its characters, and elements are trademarks
of Turner Entertainment Co. and the Stephens Mitchell Trusts." $270.00 – 300.00

Row 2:   *James Dean,* 16" high, 15" wide. Edition: 500. "HAPPY MEMORIES
COLLECTIBLES Woodland Hills, California, LIMITED EDITION
____ OF 500. ™/© 1994 James Dean Foundation under license
authorized by Curtis Management Group, Indianapolis, IN 46202
USA. MADE IN USA." Note: comes in red or blue jacket. $300.00 – 315.00

Hopalong Cassidy and Topper, 15½" high, 14½" wide with genuine
platinum-plated revolver and bridle. "Authorized and licensed by U. S.
Television Office, Inc. Design approved by Grace Bradley Boyd,
aka Mrs. Hopalong Cassidy. Limited edition: 500." $400.00+

Row 3:   *Marilyn Monroe,* 15" high, 12" wide. Edition I, wearing Classic
White 500. Edition II, wearing Stunning Pink 300. Edition III, wearing
Glamorous Teal, 300. "HAPPY MEMORIES COLLECTIBLES Woodland
Hills, California, LIMITED EDITION #____ OF 300, ©1995 The Estate
of Marilyn Monroe. All Rights Reserved. Marilyn Monroe™ (signature),
MARILYN™, AND NORMA JEANE™ are trademarks of the estate
of Marilyn Monroe. Represented by The Roger Richman AGency,
Inc. Beverly Hills, CA MADE IN USA." $300.00 – 315.00

HELEN'S WARE

Carl Gibbs accidentally uncovered the long-sought-after information about Helen Hutula and her small ceramics company. Carl worked closely with Metlox designers, Bob Allen and Mel Shaw, while researching his Metlox book. Both of these artisans worked briefly for Helen's Ware in early 1946 before joining Metlox. Bob Allen's association with Helen Hutula began slightly earlier when they collaborated on the design of the ceramic parts for two nursery lamps produced by Ray Wilcox of Fearles Camera Company in Culver City, California.

Wilcox was so impressed with Hutula's work he decided to provide financial backing for her own ceramic plant on Old San Fernando Road in Burbank, California. Helen's Ware products, many designed by herself, were hand cast. Only one firing was required because the color decoration was hand painted directly onto the greenware. Various color schemes were employed for each item with pastels, especially blue, pink, and white, predominating. Items usually bore underglaze markings in black script on the bottom. Paper identifying labels were often used as well.

The company's greatest success was the Tat-L-Tale cookie jars. Marked "© Helen's Tat-L-Tale, Helen Hutula Original" underglaze, it also had a paper label reading " I'm the Original Tat-L-Tale — Tip my head upside down." This jar featured the novel use of a voice box (crier) attached to the underside of the lid. When the lid was lifted, the crier tattled, "Ma-Ma" warning Mother her little ones were attempting to raid the cookie jar. The uplifted face and open mouth of the figure reinforced the tattletale idea. Two sizes of the female Tat-L-Tale jar, each with a few design variations were produced along with a rarer, rotund male version. Dressed in overalls, a plaid shirt, and a round brim cap, his pixie-like appearance was enhanced by winking eyes, large, almost pointed ears, hands clenched in front, and, of course, a large open mouth eager to snitch.

The use of a crier and the comical design of these jars contributed to their popularity. Bob Allen acknowledged they were the inspiration for Metlox's Calf-says Moo, Kitten-says Meow, and Lamb-says Baa cookie jars.

Other Hutula originals discovered by collectors are found in *Collector's Encyclopedia of Cookie Jars, Books I* and *II*.

Cookie Jarrin', January/February 1995

Row 1:	*Tat-L-Tale* cookie jar, "©Helen's Tat-L-Tale, Helen Hutula Original." Romberg.	$700.00 – 750.00
	Tat-L-Tale cookie jar, "©Helen's Tat-L-Tale, Helen Hutula Original." Romberg.	$750.00 – 800.00
Row 2:	*Tat-L-Tale* cookie jar, smaller size, "©Helen's Tat-L-Tale, Helen Hutula Original." Romberg.	$800.00 – 850.00
	Tat-L-Tale, cookie jar, "©Helen's Tat-L-Tale, Helen Hutula Original." Romberg.	$700.00 – 750.00

HIRSCH MANUFACTURING COMPANY

Additional jars distributed by William H. Hirsch are featured in *Book II*.

Row 1:   *Nun* cookie jar, "WH HIRSCH MFG. CO. CALIF. USA." Fralish. $275.00 – 325.00

                 Gingerbread House cookie jar, unmarked. $50.00 – 60.00

                 Gingerbread House cookie jar, unmarked. $50.00 – 60.00

Row 2:   *Treasure Chest* cookie jar, "WH © '58." $60.00 – 70.00

                 Treasure Chest cookie jar, "WH © '58." $70.00 – 80.00

                 Hobby Horse cookie jar, "19©56 WM. HIRSCH CALIFORNIA." Darrow. $175.00 – 200.00

Row 3:   *Chef* cookie jar, "WH HIRSCH MFG. CO USA LOS ANGELES CALIF." $250.00 – 275.00

                 Basketball cookie jar, "WH HIRSCH MFG. CO. MADE IN U.S.A." $100.00 – 125.00

                 Turtle cookie jar, stamped, "WILLIAM H HIRSCH MFG. CO. Los Angeles © California." $50.00 – 60.00

Below: *Rabbit* cookie jar, "WH ©'58." Darrow. $30.00 – 40.00

                 Rabbit salt and pepper set, 6⅛" high, "©1960 W.H. HIRSCH MFG. CO." $25.00 – 30.00

                 Planet cookie jar with rocket finial, "WH '55 ©." $75.00 – 85.00

Row 1:   *Cow* cookie jar, "WH Hirsch Mfg. Co. Calif. USA." Darrow. $125.00 – 150.00

   Wall Telephone cookie jar, stamped "William H. Hirsch MFG. CO
   Los Angeles, California." Potter. $90.00 – 110.00

Row 2:   *Beehive* cookie jar, 10½" high, "WH Hirsch Mfg. Made in USA."
   Darrow. $150.00 – 175.00

   Hotei cookie jar, "HIRSCH MFG. W-1 California U.S.A." Darrow. $50.00 – 60.00

Below: *Peck o' Cookies* cookie jar, back stamp "William H. Hirsch Mfg. Co
   © California." Darrow. $200.00 – 225.00

HULL POTTERY COMPANY
1905 – 1985

Below: *Gingerbread Depot* designed by Louise Bauer for Larry Taylor, last president of the Hull Pottery Company. This piece was designed to go with the Hull's Train canister set seven years after their closing. In reality, it is not Hull. Incised into bottom of jar, "hull © *Crooksville, Ohio Oven Proof U.S.A.* 1992." Antiques Mercantile, Marshfield, Mo.

$175.00 – 225.00

LARK CREATIONS

Lark Creations (Mark and Lyn Boone) commisioned this commemorative edition of the only cookie jar ever modeled after the "Car of Tomorrow," the 1948 Tucker sedan. With Mark hosting the 1997 Tucker Automobile Club of America Convention, he felt this was the perfect way to immortalize the Tucker.

The Boones collect cookie jars and Tucker memorabilia. Only 51 Tucker automobiles were ever produced, dramatically less in number than the 251 cookie jars.

Below: *Tucker Sedan,* LTD Ed., 50th Anniversary commemorative cookie
jar, "1947 – 1997 SYMBOL of SAFETY, 50 Year Commemorative Edition,
Produced by The New Rose Collection exclusively for Lark Creations,
Made in the U.S.A., A P — 1 of 251."   Issue price $151.00

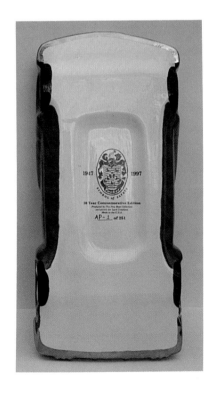

K & L ENTERPRISES

K&L Enterprises, which create limited edition cookie jars, was founded in 1995 by the mother-daughter partnership of Karen and Lorie Wuttke. Their first jar, a bison (original design), was introduced in 1996. They expanded into licensed jars in 1997 with Chuck E. Cheese. The company works closely with Clay Art in the design and production of their jars. In 1997, they acquired the sole distributorship of the Goebel *Cardinal* cookie jar.

Row 1:   *Mother's Wonder,* features and honors the folklore and rarity of a white bison calf. "K&L Enterprises 'Mother's Wonder' © 1996_____ of 600 Clay Art Made in China, designed by CA." Incised into mold. "C•A•."   Issue price $110.00

Before bison were nearly hunted to extinction in the late 1800s, bison experts estimate the odds for an albino calf being born were one in ten million.

The white buffalo is particularly sacred to the Cheyenne, Sioux, and other nomadic tribes of the Northern Plains that once relied on the buffalo for subsistence.

Legend has it a holy woman delivered a sacred pipe to the Sioux Indians then transformed it into a white buffalo — a symbol of the earth's abundance.

Bison Cow and Calf, "K&L ENTERPRISES © 1996 Clay Art Made in China, designed by CA." Incised into mold "C.A."   Issue price $80.00

Row 2:   *Chuck E. Cheese,* "K&L ENTERPRISES 'Chuck E. Cheese's 20th Anniversary' © 1997 All Rights Reserved ____ of 1977 Chuck E. Cheese and Associated Trademarks Are Owned By And Used Under License From ShowBiz Pizza Time, Inc. LICENSEE K & L ENTERPRISES Made in China DESIGNED BY Clay Art," Incised "C•A•."   Issue price (1997) $110.00

Cardinal, 1997 reissue of the *K29 "Keksdose"* Biscuit Barrel (or cookie jar) is being produced by Goebel in a limited 430-unit run under contract with Fritz Gallery, a Goebel dealer in St. Charles, Illinois.

The roly-poly cleric in cardinal form was first made by Goebel in 1960 and introduced at Great Britain's Blackpool Fair of 1961. Standing 9½" high, with his sandals and open toes, the rotund gentleman is one of the largest friars along with the *SD 37* Bank.   Issue price $465.00

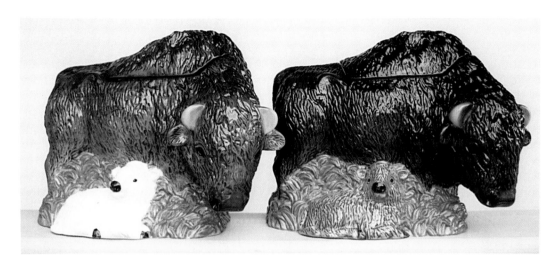

LEFTON

Lefton china was founded by Hungarian-born George Zolton Lefton in 1941. Under the leadership of second generation Leftons, this Chicago, Illinois-based importer/distributor is very much alive and well today as we rapidly approach the twenty-first century.

Row 1:   *Bluebird Love Nest* cookie jar, 11" high, "#H 7525," Paper label "Lefton TM Exclusive Japan." Horelica. $225.00 – 250.00

Boy cookie jar, 8⅜" high, "#396" on base, "Lefton Japan" on label. Blumenfeld. $200.00 – 225.00

Girl cookie jar, 8⅜" high, "397" on base, Paper label "Lefton Japan." Blumenfeld. $200.00 – 225.00

Row 2:   *French Girl* cookie jar, 9" high, "#1174" on base. Paper label "Lefton Japan." Horelica. $275.00 – 300.00

Scotch Girl cookie jar, 9" high, "#1173." Paper label "Lefton Japan." Horelica. $275.00 – 300.00

Row 3:   *Dutch Girl* jam jar, #2697." Wooldridge. $75.00 – 95.00

Dutch Girl covered sugar, "#2698." Wooldridge.   Set $75.00 – 95.00

Dutch Girl cookie jar, "#2366." Wooldridge. $175.00 – 225.00

Dutch Girl creamer, "#2698." Wooldridge.   Set $75.00 – 95.00

Below: *Bossie Cow* cookie jar, "#6594." Darrow. $125.00 – 150.00

Bossie Cow pitcher, "#6515." Darrow. $30.00 – 35.00

Bossie Cow bowl, "#6515." Darrow. $25.00 – 30.00

McCOY

Row 1:
   Slant-top Tepee, embossed "McCoy USA 137." Lindberg. $275.00 – 325.00

   Basket of Eggs, incised "0274 LCC USA." Lindberg. $40.00 – 50.00

   Coke Jug with under-glaze flower design (unusual decoration), unmarked. Lindberg. $50.00 – 60.00

Row 2:
   Kid's Stuff Cat, unusual decoration (Designer Accents), "1502 USA." Lindberg. $35.00 – 45.00

   Wren House, v-top/split roof, brown bird, "McCoy USA." Hard to find version. Lindberg. $550.00 – 600.00

   Cookies canister, brown drip glaze. "Kathy Kale" incised in circle. Unusual mark. Lindberg. $25.00 – 30.00

Row 3:
   Drum Majorette, "McCoy." Demory.   Too rare to price.

Below:
   Split-Trunk Elephant (yellow), "McCoy." Rare coloration. Rhinehimer. $350.00 – 400.00

   Dan the Dog (with original box), "USA ALPO DAN THE DOG." Coley. $65.00 – 75.00

Row 1: *Hocus Rabbit* (brown drip), incised "211 LCC McCoy USA."
Prestwood. $75.00 – 85.00

Christmas cylinder. Prestwood. $150.00+

Christmas bell, McCoy Limited. Prestwood.   Price not determined.

Row 2: *Brown Rose* cylinder, embossed "McCoy USA." Hard to find. Lindberg. $70.00 – 80.00

Lost Glaze cylinder, embossed "McCoy USA." Hard to find. Lindberg. $125.00 – 150.00

Blue flowers cylinder (under glaze), embossed "McCoy USA." Hard
to find. Lindberg. $60.00 – 70.00

Row 3: *Pearl Cascade* cylinder, embossed "McCoy USA." Hard to find. Lindberg. $60.00 – 70.00

Brown Drip cylinder, embossed "USA 28." Lindberg. $30.00 – 40.00

Green Stripes/Pebble Surface cylinder, embossed "McCoy USA."
Hard to find. Lindberg. $125.00 – 150.00

Below: *Bareheaded Cookie Boy,* "NM USA." Rare. Demory.   Price not determined.

Basketball, unmarked. Rare. Moloney.   Price not determined.

Row 1:   *Grandma's Cookies,* Designer Accents, "USA 1008." Lindberg. $30.00 – 35.00

Flying Ducks (Mallards), unmarked Designer Accents. Lindberg. $30.00 – 35.00

Carved Tulips, Designer Accents, "4251 USA." Lindberg. $30.00 – 35.00

Row 2:   *Old Strawberry* (white drip), embossed, "McCoy USA." Lindberg. $50.00 – 60.00

Pirate Chest, incised "252 McCoy USA." Lindberg. $125.00 – 150.00

New Strawberry, incised "263 USA." Lindberg. $30.00 – 40.00

Row 3:   *Clown in barrel,* embossed "McCoy USA." Hard-to-find color. Lindberg. $125.00 – 150.00

Barnum's Animals blank, incised "152 USA." Lindberg. $45.00 – 55.00

Rooster, embossed "McCoy USA." Lindberg. $75.00 – 95.00

Below: *Soccer ball,* unmarked. Rare. Demory.   Price not determined.

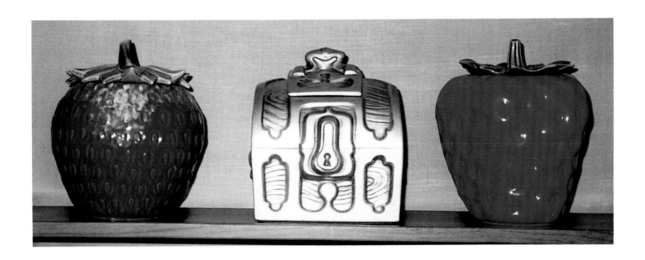

Row 1:   *Gypsy Pot*, embossed "7531 McCoy USA." Lindberg. $35.00 – 45.00

Kookie Kettle, white w/brown rose, hard to find, embossed
"McCoy USA." Lindberg. $170.00 – 180.00

Gypsy Pot, unmarked. Lindberg. $35.00 – 45.00

Row 2:   *Pink Flowers* canister, incised "McCoy LCC USA." Lindberg. $30.00 – 40.00

Owl, incised "204 USA." $40.00 – 45.00

Tea Party canister, incised "McCoy LCC USA." Lindberg. $50.00 – 60.00

Row 3:   *Hot Air Balloon*, incised "353 USA." $40.00 – 50.00

Engine with smoke, unmarked. Rare. Lindberg.   Price not determined.

Hot Air Balloon, incised "353 USA." Lindberg. $40.00 – 50.00

Below: *Engine with smoke*, unmarked. Rare. Moloney.   Price not determined.

Engine with smoke, unmarked. Rare. Timmerman.   Price not determined.

Row 1: *'76 Milk Can,* "7019 LCC McCoy USA." Lindberg. $30.00 – 40.00

'76 Milk Can, "USA." Lindberg. $30.00 – 40.00

'76 Milk Can, "USA." Lindberg. $30.00 – 40.00

Row 2: *Happy Times* milk can, "From the Littlest Things, Great Happiness Springs," incised "9 USA." Lindberg. $40.00 – 50.00

Bobby Baker, low hat, incised "183." Lindberg. $50.00 – 60.00

Antique Dutchland milk can, incised "USA." Lindberg. $55.00 – 65.00

Row 3: *Apple,* flat leaves, unmarked. Hard to find. Lindberg. $75.00 – 100.00

Pear, flat leaves, unmarked. Hard to find. Lindberg. $100.00 – 125.00

Apple, serrated leaf, embossed "USA McCoy." Hard to find, Lindberg. $75.00 – 85.00

Below: *Pear, with Pussy Finial* (from Pussy at the Well planter), unmarked, 9½" high. One-of-a-kind. Eggert/Seman. Price not determined.

Pear, flat leaves, 10½" high, unmarked. Hard to find. Eggert/Seman. $100.00 – 125.00

Apple, flat leaves, 7½" high, unmarked. Hard to find. Eggert/Seman. $75.00 – 100.00

Row 1:	*Ball* with hand-painted flowers, unmarked. Lindberg.	$25.00 – 35.00
	Fortune Cookies, gold stripes, embossed "McCoy USA." Hard to find. Lindberg.	$75.00 – 100.00
	Ball with hand-painted flowers, unmarked. Lindberg.	$25.00 – 35.00
Row 2:	*Jug,* small with actual cork, unmarked, 3-banded foot. Lindberg.	$30.00 – 40.00
	Jug, large with actual cork, unmarked, 3-banded foot. Sticker says "Cookies." Lindberg.	$30.00 – 40.00
	Jug, small with ceramic cork, embossed "McCoy USA." Lindberg.	$30.00 – 40.00
Row 3:	*Teapot,* speckled tan, incised "219 McCoy USA."	$60.00 – 70.00
	Milk Can reproduction, incised "Authentic McCoy Reproductions by McCoy circa 1911."	$50.00 – 60.00
	Teapot, incised "219 McCoy USA." Lindberg.	$60.00 – 70.00
Below:	*Frosted Christmas Tree,* embossed "McCoy USA." Honchar.	$800.00+
	Christmas Teddy (minus friend), 11½" high, "154 USA." Eggert/Seman.	Price not determined.
	Christmas Chilly Willy, 11¾" high, "154 USA." Eggert/Seman.	Price not determined.

Row 1:   *Round Hobnail,* rectangular finial, unmarked. Lindberg. $150.00 – 175.00

Round Hobnail, hard-to-find color, unmarked. Lindberg. $200.00 – 225.00

Round Hobnail, unmarked. Lindberg. $175.00 – 200.00

Row 2:   *Heart-shaped Hobnail,* unmarked. Lindberg. $350.00 – 400.00

Kissing Penguins, rare color, embossed "McCoy." Lindberg.   Price not determined.

Round Hobnail, hard to find color, unmarked. Lindberg. $200.00 – 225.00

Row 3:   *Crayola Kids* canister, hobby or stick horse, incised "McCoy LCC USA." Lindberg. $65.00 – 75.00

New Pineapple, embossed "USA." Lindberg. $75.00 – 85.00

Crayola Kids with ball canister, incised "McCoy LCC USA." Lindberg. $65.00 – 75.00

Below: *Round hobnail,* unmarked. Moloney. $75.00 – 100.00

Heart-shaped Hobnail, unmarked. Moloney. $350.00 – 400.00

Round Hobnail, unmarked. Moloney. $175.00 – 225.00

Row 2:   *Heart-shaped Hobnail,* unmarked. Moloney. $325.00 – 375.00

Heart-shaped Hobnail, unmarked. Moloney. $325.00 – 375.00

Heart-shaped Hobnail, unmarked. Moloney. $400.00 – 425.00

Heart-shaped Hobnail, unmarked. Moloney. $375.00 – 400.00

Row 1:   *Kitten on Coal Bucket,* prototype, colors not used in regular production. Demory. $325.00 – 375.00

                Gleep, multicolor, unmarked. Demory.   Price not determined.

Row 2:   *School Bus,* unmarked experimental jar. Demory.   Too rare to value.

                Covered Wagon, gold burst. Demory.   Price not determined.

Row 3:   *W. C. Fields,* unmarked. Demory. $250.00 – 275.00

                Grape Press unmarked experimental. Demory.   Too rare to value.

Below: *Leprechaun,* cold paint, unmarked. Hard to find. Davis. $1,000.00+

                Leprechaun, cold paint, unmarked. Hard to find. Lindberg. $1,000.00+

Row 1:   *Honey Bear,* "McCoy USA." Prestwood. $150.00 – 175.00

            Mouse on Clock, unmarked. Prestwood. $150.00 – 175.00

            Kissing Penguins, "McCoy."   Price not determined.

Row 2:   *Flower Pot with Plastic Flowers,* "McCoy." Prestwood. $450.00+

            Kookie Kettle, white with brown rose, hard to find. Embossed. "McCoy USA." Prestwood. $170.00 – 180.00

            Anytime is Cookie Time cylinder, "McCoy USA." Prestwood. $65.00 – 75.00

Row 3:   *Round with Gold Trim,* gold lid, "USA." Demory.   Price not determined.

            Aqua cylinder, "McCoy USA." Prestwood. $50.00 – 60.00

            Black with Flower Panels, modern cylinder, 1970 – 71, "254 McCoy, USA." Prestwood. $30.00 – 40.00

Below: *Santa,* 21¼" high, 38½" around, "McCoy LTD." Originally made for Wicks 'n Sticks, selling wholesale for $45.00. The survival rate of one in ten pieces halted production. Less than 50 (probably no more than 30) were ever produced. Curtis. $1,000.00+

            Turkey cookie/candy jar by McCoy Limited. Prestwood.   Price not determined.

            Pumpkin cookie/candy jar by McCoy Limited. Prestwood.   Price not determined.

            Buccaneer stoneware pretel jar. Prestwood. $100.00 – 150.00

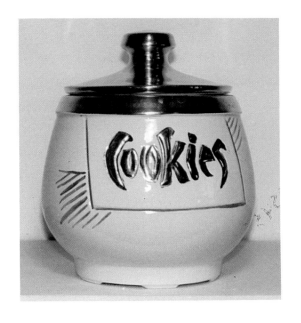

McME PRODUCTIONS

Lonna McGee and Gerald Meyer launched McMe Productions with their *Bell Captain* cookie jar in 1992 (see *Black Americana Book II*). Moving into the area of Western collectibles and licensed items, they brought out Roy Rogers, Dale Evans, Roy and Trigger, and Gene Autry. Laurel and Hardy were introduced in 1996; the Three Stooges were added in 1997. All items are produced in the United States.

In addition to the jars featured on these pages, *Uncle Justin* and *Florence Mildred, Allie Rebecca's* playmate, can be found in the Black Americana chapter.

Row 1:   Roy Rogers signing model of Roy.

Roy Rogers, red fired-on decal, "Mc/Me" within heart, "Produced by Mc Me Productions Simi Valley, CA Made in Southern California ©1994 Roy Rogers Enterprises Limited Edition ———/2500." Signed across the back of original model by Roy, the impression is highlighted with fired gold. Discontinued. Less than 1,300 pieces produced.   Issue price $159.00

Row 2:   *Trigger,* red decal, "TRIGGER The Horse That Made Roy Rogers Famous Produced by Mc Me Productions Simi Valley, CA 93063 Under license of the Roy Rogers & Dale Evans Museum ©1995 No. ____/1933."   Issue price $225.00

Roy Rogers signing model of *Trigger.*

Below: *Dale Evans,* red fired-on decal, "Mc/Me" within heart, "Produced by Mc Me Productions Simi Valley, CA Made in Southern California ©1994 Roy Rogers Enterprises Limited Edition ___/2500." Incised into mold another heart with "Mc/Me, Mc Me Productions, SIMI VALLEY, CA MADE IN SO CA ©1994 ROY ROGERS ENTERPRISES." Signed across the back of original model by Dale, the impression is highlighted with fired gold. Discontinued. Fewer than 400 pieces produced.   Issue price $159.00

Row 1:   _Gene Autry_ cookie jar prototype.   Value not determined.

                    Gene Autry, "©1995 AUTRY MUSEUM of WESTERN HERITAGE, GENE AUTRY THE SINGING COWBOY, Mc Me PRODUCTIONS, SIMI VALLEY, CA." and "McMe" within the shape of a heart. "___/1000" written on glaze in fired gold. Gene Autry signed the model across the back, the impression is highlighted with fired gold.   Issue price $195.00

Row 2:   Gene Autry signing model of Gene.

Below: _Cathy,_ back of jar signed by "Cathy Guisewite." Incised into bottom of the base, "CATHY ©1994 GUISEWITE STUDIO, Mc/Me (in heart), (#___ written on glaze in fired gold), McMe Productions, Simi Valley, CA, MADE IN SO CALIFORNIA USA." Discontinued. Approx. 400 pieces produced.   Issue price $150.00

                    Cathy Guisewite signing _Cathy_ model.

Row 1:   *Oliver Hardy,* "___/1000 Oliver Hardy ™ & © 1996 Larry Harman
Pictures Corp. ©Larry Harman Pictures Corp. Hollywood, CA 90028,"
the shape of a heart with "Mc/Me," and "Mc/McProductions, Simi
Valley, CA 93063 Made in the U.S.A." Signed, "Oliver Hardy" across
the back of the trunk on which Ollie sits.   Issue price $125.00

Stan Laurel, "___/1000 Stan Laurel™ & © 1996 Larry Harman
Pictures Corp. ©Larry Harman Pictures Corp. Hollywood, CA
90028," the shape of a heart with "Mc/Me" and "McMe Productions,
Simi Valley, CA 93063 Made in the U.S.A." Signed, "Stan Laurel"
across the back of trunk on which Stan sits.   Issue price $125.00

Row 2:   *Larry,* "TM & © 1996 Comedy III PRODUCTIONS INC., ALL RIGHTS
RESERVED Mc/Me PRODUCTIONS SIMI VALLEY, CA MADE IN U.S.A.
____/600." Incised within heart-shaped impression, "Mc/Me."   Issue price $130.00

Curly, "TM & © 1996 Comedy III PRODUCTIONS INC., ALL RIGHTS
RESERVED Mc/Me PRODUCTIONS SIMI VALLEY, CA MADE IN U.S.A.
____/600." Incised within heart-shaped impression, "Mc/Me."   Issue price $130.00

Moe, TM & © 1996 Comedy III PRODUCTIONS INC., ALL RIGHTS
RESERVED Mc/Me PRODUCTIONS SIMI VALLEY, CA MADE IN U.S.A.
____/600." Incised within heart-shaped impression, "Mc/Me."   Issue price $130.00

Below: *Allie Rebecca,* with buggy, limited edition of 250 jars, each approx.
14" high.   Issue price $125.00

Hopalong Cassidy cookie jar model, available in two editions. The
gold edition, strictly limited to 250 jars, wears a wine-colored scarf
and has fired gold scarf slide.   Issue price $195.00
   Regular edition, dressed with blue scarf and bone-colored scarf
slide, limited to a maximum of 1,000 jars.   Issue price $135.00

METLOX

Row 1:   *Owl,* 9⅜" high, "MADE IN POPPYTRAIL CALIF." Horelica. $40.00 – 50.00

Dina (Stegosaurus), 9⅞", "METLOX CALIF. USA BY VINCENT." Hard to find. Horelica. $175.00 – 200.00

Row 2:   *Wells Fargo Stagecoach,* "Made in California" in script. There is also a bisque version of the Wells Fargo Stagecoach (not show). $625.00 – 675.00

Hobby Horse, unmarked. $600.00 – 650.00

Row 3:   *Santa,* chocolate, 14¼" high, "METLOX CALIF. USA." Rare. Horelica. $850.00+

Easter Bunny, 13⅝", "METLOX CALIF, USA". Rare. Horelica. $325.00 – 375.00

Easter Bunny, chocolate, 13⅝" high, "METLOX CALIF. USA." Rare. Horelica. $750.00+

Below: *Santa* (Terra Madre), 14⅛" high, stamped "Original California Pottery by Metlox ©," incised "METLOX CALIF USA." Rare.   Price not determined.

Row 1:	*Rabbit* salt or pepper shaker, unmarked.	$30.00 – 40.00
	Cabbage salt and pepper set, unmarked.	$25.00 – 35.00
	Rabbit salt or pepper shaker, unmarked.	$30.00 – 40.00
Row 2:	*Rabbit* bank, unmarked.	$65.00 – 75.00
	Cabbage salt and pepper set, unmarked.	$25.00 – 35.00
Row 3:	*Rabbit* (with carrot), "MADE IN USA."	$600.00 – 650.00
	Flash (turtle), "METLOX CALIF. USA."	$600.00 – 650.00
	Rabbit (with carrot), stained, not glazed, "METLOX CALIF USA." Potter.	$275.00 – 325.00
Below:	*Dottie* (Hippo), 7½" high, 13½" long, unmarked. Hard to find. Horelica.	$625.00 – 675.00

Row 1: *Beau Bear* canister (small), 8⅞" high, "METLOX CALIF. USA."
Hard to find. $75.00 – 95.00

Beau Bear double-handle mug, "METLOX CALIF. USA." $50.00 – 60.00

Beau Bear salt and pepper set, unmarked. $25.00 – 35.00

Row 2: *Beau Bear* large canister with yellow bow, "Metlox W11758" under glaze.
Beckerson. $125.00 – 150.00

Beau Bear large canister with blue bow, "Metlox." Beckerson. $125.00 – 150.00

Teddy Bear lamp (one-piece mold). Beckerson. $65.00 – 75.00

Row 3: *Humpty Dumpty* children's ware, "METLOX CALIFORNIA POTTERY
U.S.A." $35.00 – 45.00

Proud Bear plate, "THE PROUD BEAR PLATE THE ORIGINAL RED
PLATE CO. – CALIFORNIA, U.S.A. HAND DECORATED ©1993." $50.00 – 60.00

Below: *Topsy* yellow apron with blue band. Beckerson. $600.00 – 650.00

Row 1:   *Grapefruit,* "MADE IN USA." $150.00 – 175.00

Basket with Lemon Lid, "MADE IN Poppytrail CALIF." (Poppytrail, superimposed over an outline of California.) $100.00 – 125.00

Orange (or grapefruit?), "MADE IN USA." $55.00 – 65.00

Row 2:   *Artichoke* from Terra Madre line. $100.00 – 120.00

Broccoli from Terra Madre line. $90.00 – 110.00

Corn from Terra Madre line. $90.00 – 110.00

Row 3:   *Owl* small canister, 6¾" high, incised "MADE IN POPPYTRAIL CALIF."   3-piece set $100.00 – 125.00

Owl medium canister, 8⅜" high, incised "MADE IN POPPYTRAIL CALIF."   3-piece set $100.00 – 125.00

Owl large canister, 9⅛" high, incised "MADE IN POPPYTRAIL CALIF."   3-piece set $100.00 – 125.00

Below: *Pear,* 10⅜" high, incised "MADE IN USA." $175.00 – 200.00

Mushroom House, "MADE IN Poppytrail CALIF. U.S.A." (Poppytrail, superimposed over an outline of California.) $325.00 – 375.00

Row 1:   *Noah's Ark,* bisque with glaze accent, "Made in Poppytrail Calif." $70.00 – 90.00

            Tulip Time 2-qt. canister with wooden lid. Beckerson. $60.00 – 90.00

Row 2:   *Frosty Penguin,* long coat, "Metlox Calif. U.S.A." Darrow. $100.00 – 125.00

            Frosty Penguin, short coat, "Metlox Calif. U.S.A." Darrow. $125.00 – 150.00

Row 3:   *Sammy Seal,* "Metlox Calif. U.S.A." $750.00+

            Sammy Seal salt and pepper set, "Metlox Calif. U.S.A." $125.00 – 150.00

            Lighthouse, unmarked. Darrow. $325.00 – 375.00

Below: *Itaglio,* 10" high, unmarked. Candee. $175.00 – 200.00

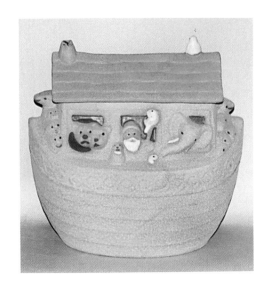

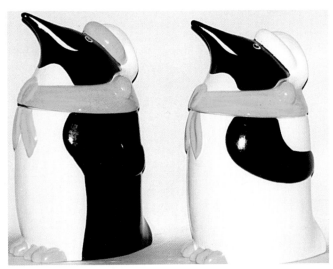

Row 1:   *Egg Basket,* "METLOX MADE IN U.S.A." $125.00 – 150.00

Cock-A-Doodle-Do canister, paper label. Beckerson. $100.00 – 125.00

Hen and Rooster salt and pepper set from Cock-A-Doodle-Do line.
Beckerson. $25.00 – 35.00

Row 2:   *Hen,* off-white with green trim. Beckerson.   Price not determined.

Hen on Nest salt or pepper shaker, unmarked.   Set $25.00 – 35.00

Chick salt and pepper set, unmarked.   Set $25.00 – 35.00

Hen on Nest salt or pepper shaker, unmarked.   Set $25.00 – 35.00

Row 3:   *Rooster,* "Made in Poppytrail Calif." Potter.   Price not determined.

Rooster, "Made in Poppytrail Calif." $275.00 – 325.00

Below: *Turkey,* 14" x 13" wide. Beckerson. $600.00 – 650.00

Hen with Chick, paper label "METLOX MANUFACTURING CO." $500.00 – 550.00

Row 1: *Holstein Calf* (Ferdinand), made for Johnny Carson show, "Metlox Calif USA." Beckerson.   Price not determined.

White Face or Purple Herford, with bell. Beckerson.   Price not determined.

Row 2: *Fido*, white and beige, "Made in Poppytrail U.S.A." $100.00 – 125.00

Eagle Provincial (second series), gold trim. The red is cold paint (paint which will wash off). Unmarked. Beckerson. $100.00 – 125.00

Row 3: *Schoolhouse*, paper label on front, no permanent marks. Guffy. $300.00 – 325.00

Margarita (Terra Madre line), "Metlox Calif. USA ©87 by Vincent." Guffey. $300.00 – 325.00

Below: *Lady of Spain.* This design is probably a result of early Spanish influence in California. Unmarked. Due to the enclosed lid and similarities to the *Debutante,* it is believed this jar was produced either at Evan K. Shaw's American Pottery or Metlox. $500.00 – 550.00

Debutante, plaid dress, unmarked. "The fascinating history of the Debutante jar began at a small ceramic pottery on San Fernando Boulevard owned and operated by the family of Metlox modeler, Frank Irwin. The jar was designed by the young Irwin as part of his family's nursery rhyme line produced in the late 1930s. When the Irwins joined Evan K. Shaw at American Pottery, the line was continued in production. Shaw demonstrated his appreciation of the jar by manufacturing it through the late 1940s after his purchase of Metlox." *Collector's Encyclopedia of Metlox Potteries Identification and Values* by Carl Gibbs Jr. $600.00 – 650.00

Row 1: *Geranium Basket,* unmarked. Beckerson. $100.00 – 125.00

Squirrel on Pine Cone (green lid). Beckerson. $125.00 – 150.00

Row 2: *California Geranium,* 11½" high, "Made in USA." Azzam. $100.00 – 125.00

Squash (white), paper label. Beckerson. $125.00 – 150.00

Row 3: *Pepper* (white), paper label. Beckerson. $65.00 – 75.00

Pepper, red. $75.00 – 85.00

Below: Metlox catalog sheet.

SOPHISTICATED COOKIE JARS

Beautiful in natural colors — they have a variety of uses in a variety of rooms.

Row 1:   *Carousel,* paper label. Mouton. $350.00 – 375.00

Row 2:   *Clown* (blue trim), 12¾" high, "Metlox Made in USA." Horelica. $225.00 – 275.00

             Clown (red suit). Hamburg.   Price not determined.

Below: *Poodle,* "MADE IN POPPYTRAIL CALIF. USA."   Price not determined.

             Elephant with straw hat, unmarked. $650.00 – 675.00

             Display plaque, "Vernon ware FINE DINNERWARE METLOX POTTERIES." $70.00 – 80.00

NEW SHAWNEE POTTERY COMPANY

Cecil Rapp founded his New Shawnee Pottery Company in 1994 after collecting Shawnee Pottery for several years. The decision to use the Shawnee name was born of appreciation for their style and quality and the respect the name commands in the market place.

Through years of collecting Shawnee and hearing people wonder why there was never a Farmer Pig cookie jar made to match the salt and pepper shakers, it seemed natural Farmer Pig™ should be the first jar.

Row 1: *Farmer™ Pig,* marked in black underglaze "____/500" embossed, "Shawnee" incised in script, "Farmer" followed with embossed "U.S.A."   Issue price $175.00

Sowly™ Pig and Farmer™ Pig salt and pepper set, 5⅜" and 5¼" high, "____/500 Shawnee." Paper label, "Shawnee CHINA UNDERGLAZE •HAND•DECORATED."   Set issue price $75.00

Sowly™ Pig, marked in black underglaze "____/500" embossed, "Shawnee" incised in script, "Sowly©" followed with embossed "U.S.A."   Issue price $175.00

Row 2: *Farmer™ Pig* bank/cookie jar (introduced in 1995), in black underglaze "____/100," embossed "Shawnee," then incised in script "Farmer©," followed with an embossed "U.S.A."   Issue price $175.00

Sowly™ Pig bank/cookie jar (introduced in 1995), in black underglaze "____/100" embossed, "Shawnee" incised in script, "Sowly©" followed with embossed "U.S.A."   Issue price $175.00

Below: *Billy™ in Dad's Sheriff Uniform,* issued in a limited edition of 250 hand-decorated cookie jars. The hat bands with matching handkerchiefs come in five colors, 50 of each. Each piece is marked "____/250 Shawnee Billy© U.S.A."   Issue price $175.00.

Row 1:   *Rabbit* bank, embossed on bottom "Shawnee" with a tomahawk, the trademark of New Shawnee. Though this bank is in the likeness of an original Shawnee figurine, the original stood approximately 2½" high and was unmarked. This new Shawnee piece is marked and stands 4¾" high. In addition, Shawnee never made a rabbit bank. Sold in numbered sets of 250.   Issue price for set $200.00

Squirrel bank, embossed on bottom "Shawnee" with a tomahawk, the trademark of New Shawnee. Though this bank is in the likeness of an original Shawnee figurine, the original stood approximately 2½" high and was unmarked. This new Shawnee piece is marked and stands 5⅝" high. In addition, Shawnee never made a squirrel bank. Sold in numbered sets of 250.   Issue price for set $200.00

Row 2:   *Pekinese* bank, embossed on bottom "Shawnee" with a tomahawk, the trademark of New Shawnee. Though this bank is in the likeness of an original Shawnee figurine, the original stood approximately 2½" high and was unmarked. This new Shawnee piece is marked and stands 3⅛" high. In addition, Shawnee never made a Pekinese bank. Sold in numbered sets of 250.   Issue price for set $200.00

Puppy bank, embossed on bottom "Shawnee" with a tomahawk, the trademark of New Shawnee. Though this bank is in the likeness of an original Shawnee figurine, the original stood approximately 3" high and was unmarked. This new Shawnee piece is marked and stands 5" high. In addition, Shawnee never made a squirrel bank. Sold in numbered sets of 250.   Issue price for set $200.00

Row 3:   *Deer* bank, embossed on bottom "Shawnee" with a tomahawk, the trademark of New Shawnee. Though this bank is in the likeness of an original Shawnee figurine, the original stood approximately 3" high and was unmarked. This new Shawnee piece is marked and stands 4¾" high. In addition, Shawnee never made a deer bank. Sold in numbered sets of 250.   Issue price for set $200.00

Raccoon bank, embossed on bottom "Shawnee" with a tomahawk, the trademark of New Shawnee. Though this bank is in the likeness of an original Shawnee figurine, the original stood approximately 3" high and was unmarked. This new Shawnee piece is marked and stands 4¾" high. Sold in numbered sets of 250.   Issue price for set $200.00

NORTH AMERICAN CERAMICS

North American Ceramics made many high quality, well-designed cookie jars. Additional examples can be found in *Books I and II.*

Row 1:   *Airplane* with movable propeller, unmarked. Hennessy. $575.00 – 625.00

Row 2:   *Engine,* "DCJ32 ©1987, NAC USA." $60.00 – 70.00

            Double-decker Bus, "PICCADILLY CIRCUS" on opposite side panel, "STATE STREET, Marshall Field's" on back. $350.00 – 375.00

Row 3:   *Corvette,* "ACC J9 ©1986, NAC USA" impressed into the bottom of the base in a circular design. $125.00 – 150.00

            Mercedes, "ACC J9 ©1986, NAC USA" impressed into the bottom of the base in a circular design. $100.00 – 125.00

Below: *Motorcycle with Rider,* transparent label, "DAVE DEAL ©COPYRIGHT 1988." On gold-colored label, "THIS ITEM IS INDIVIDUALLY HANDPAINTED. BRUSHED STROKES AND COLOR VARIATIONS ATTEST TO THIS UNIQUE QUALITY." $750.00+

ROSEVILLE

All jars are 8" tall.

Row 1:   *Water Lily* (pink/green), "Roseville U.S.A. 1-8." Honchar. $475.00 – 525.00

                 Water Lily (brown), "Roseville U.S.A. 1-8." Honchar. $425.00 – 475.00

                 Water Lily (blue), "Roseville U.S.A. 1-8." Honchar. $450.00 – 500.00

Row 2:   *Magnolia* (green), "Roseville U.S.A. 2-8." Honchar. $425.00 – 475.00

                 Magnolia (brown/tan), "Roseville U.S.A. 2-8." Honchar. $400.00 – 450.00

                 Magnolia (blue), "Roseville U.S.A. 2-8." Honchar. $475.00 – 525.00

Row 3:   *Clematis* (green), "Roseville U.S.A. 3-8." Honchar. $375.00 – 425.00

                 Clematis (brown), "Roseville U.S.A. 3-8." Honchar. $325.00 – 375.00

                 Clematis (blue), "Roseville U.S.A. 3-8." Honchar. $400.00 – 450.00

Row 1: Mark of Freesia. All jars are marked alike with the exception of company assigned number. Honchar.

Row 2: *Freesia* (green), "Roseville U.S.A. 4-8." Honchar. $450.00 – 500.00

  Freesia (tangerine), "Roseville U.S.A. 4-8." Honchar. $350.00 – 400.00

  Freesia (blue), "Roseville U.S.A. 4-8." Honchar. $450.00 – 500.00

Row 3: *Zephyr Lily* (green), "Roseville U.S.A. 5-8." Honchar. $475.00 – 525.00

  Zephyr Lily (brown), "Roseville U.S.A. 5-8." Honchar. $450.00 – 500.00

  Zephyr Lily (blue), "Roseville U.S.A. 5-8." Honchar. $525.00 – 575.00

SIERRA VISTA

Additional Sierra Vista cookie jars are found in *Books I* and *II.*

Row 1:   *Cockatoo*, "Sierra Vista Ceramics Pasadena Calif. © 56." Azaam.
                Not enough samples have surfaced to accurately determine value.

Row 2:   *Clown*, "Sierra Vista Ceramics ©1958 Pasadena Calif. U.S.A." Azaam.
                Not enough samples have surfaced to accurately determine value.

            Elephant, "Sierra Vista California." Potter. $125.00 – 150.00

Below: *Davy Crockett* bank. Rhinehimer. $400.00 – 450.00

            Davy Crockett cookie jar, "Sierra Vista of Calif. ©." Rhinehimer. $1,500.00+

SIGMA

Sigma was a New York based importer/distributor that started in the late 1960s as the gift ware division of Rockville International in Garden City, New York. The company eventually became part of Towle International, closing in 1985. For approximately 10 years the collaboration between Japanese factories and American designers was magical for Sigma, never again to be duplicated. Towle remains a viable conglomerate today, owning among others, International Silver.

As collectors we know the importance of fact versus guess or assumption. We are delighted to have had access to Sigma catalog sheets, finally giving some perspective to this company which was a leader in Sesame Street and Star Wars products.

Row 1: *Hortense* cookie jar, "HORTENSE Tastesetter © by Sigma designed by David Straus. Darrow. $150.00 – 175.00

Agatha, "AGATHA, Tastesetter by Sigma, designed by David Straus." Darrow. $175.00 – 200.00

Victoria, "VICTORIA, Tastesetter by Sigma, designed by David Straus." Darrow. $200.00 – 255.00

Millicent cookie jar, "MILLICENT Tastesetter © Sigma designed by David Straus. Darrow. $225.00 – 250.00

Row 2: *Ringmaster* covered box, "Circus by David Straus for Tastesetter © Sigma." Darrow. $65.00 – 75.00

Fat Lady, "CIRCUS David Straus" in mold. "Tastesetter ©Sigma, PLEASE NOTE THAT ALL PIECES ARE HAND DECORATED, SO COLOR VARIANCE COULD OCCUR. LABORATORY TESTED TO COMPLY WITH FDA GUIDELINES, Made in Japan." Darrow. $175.00 – 200.00

Strong Man covered box, "CIRCUS by David Straus for Tastesetter © Sigma." Darrow. $65.00 – 70.00

Row 3: *Popcorn Vendor,* "Tastesetter by Sigma" on paper label. Darrow. $450.00+

Senorita, "SIESTA Tastesetter by Sigma Designed by David Straus." Darrow. $300.00 – 350.00

Below: *Circus Train* canister set, "CIRCUS by DAVID STRAUS © SIGMA the Tastesetter." Potter. $150.00 – 175.00

Row 1:   *Santa* cookie jar, "Sigma the Tastesetter®© MCMLXXXIV." Saxton. $75.00 – 95.00

                Fat Cat, "FAT CAT Sigma Tastesetter MCMLXXXV." McNab. $300.00 – 325.00

Row 2:   *Mrs. Tiggy-Winkle,* from the *Tale of Mrs. Tiggy-Winkle* by Beatrix Potter. Illustrated by Allen Atkinson, "©MCMLXXXIII Sigma the Tastesetter." Darrow. $325.00 – 350.00

                Last Elegant Bear tissue holder. Darrow. $50.00 – 60.00

Row 3:   *Panda Chef,* "Cara Marks for Sigma the Tastesetter." Darrow. $75.00 – 95.00

                Peter Rabbit cookie jar, Peter Rabbit from the *Tales of Peter Rabbit* by Beatrix Potter. Illustrated by Allen Atkinson, "©MCMLXXXIII Sigma the Tastesetter." Darrow. $150.00 – 175.00

                W.C. Fields bank, incised, "©W.C. Fields Prod. © Sigma." $65.00 – 75.00

Below: *Chick,* "CHICK CARA MARKS FOR Sigma the Tastesetter." McNab. $75.00 – 95.00

                Snowman, "SNOWMAN by DENNIS KYTE For Sigma TASTESETTER." McNab. $100.00 – 125.00

Row 1:   *Theodora Dog* (dog) biscuit container, "Theodora Taste Setter ©
by Sigma." Darrow. $125.00 – 150.00

Cubs Bear cookie jar, "Krazy Kids and Kritters David Hyman for
Sigma the Tastesetter © MCMLXXXIV." Darrow. $125.00 – 150.00

Row 2:   *Rag Doll* cookie jar "Sigma the Tastesetter © MCMLXXXIV." Potter. $200.00 – 225.00

Ballerina Cat cookie jar, "Krazy Kids and Kritters David Hyman for
Sigma the Tastesetter © MCMLXXXIV." Darrow. $250.00 – 275.00

Elephant with Ball and Glove, "CARA MARKS for Sigma the
Tastesetter®." Darrow. $125.00 – 150.00

Row 3:   *Chef with Dog* cookie jar, "Sigma the Tastesetter © MCMLXXXIV."
Darrow. $75.00 – 95.00

Chef canister, "Les Artisans Sigma the Tastesetter © MCMLXXXIV ®
Towle Company." Darrow. $60.00 – 75.00

Village canister, "Tastesetter by Sigma." Darrow. $45.00 – 55.00

Below: *Duck* canister, "The Decorative Kitchen™ Duck by Sigma the Tastesetter
© MCMLXXXII ® Towle Company." Darrow. $35.00 – 45.00

Goose, on paper label "Tastesetter by Sigma Made in Italy #53."
Darrow. $75.00 – 95.00

Rabbit cylinder, "The Decorative Kitchen™ Rabbit by Sigma the
Tastesetter © MCMLXXXII ® Towle Company." Darrow. $35.00 – 45.00

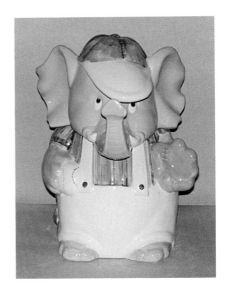

Row 1: *Wind in the Willows,* "THE WIND IN THE WILLOWS© ARIEL Inc. '81 ©
Sigma the Tastesetter™." Darrow. $125.00 – 150.00

Gloria Vanderbilt *Cabbage,* "HAND PAINTED, MADE IN BRAZIL,
Tastesetter Sigma" on paper label. Darrow. $65.00 – 75.00

Row 2: *Beaver Fireman,* "CARA MARKS for Sigma the Tastesetter." $250.00 – 275.00

Pig Clown, "CARA MARKS for Sigma the Tastesetter." Potter. $175.00 – 200.00

Row 3: *Pig Chef,* "Sigma the Tastesetter.®" $100.00 – 125.00

Fat Cat, "©Sigma the Tastesetter," paper label "Tastesetter © Sigma,
PLEASE NOTE THAT ALL PIECES ARE HAND DECORATED, SO COLOR
VARIANCE COULD OCCUR. LABORATORY TESTED TO COMPLY
WITH FDA GUIDELINES, Made in Japan." Boshears. $450.00+

Below: *Kabuki Dancer,* "KABUKI © Sigma the Tastesetter." Darrow. $125.00 – 175.00

Kabuki covered box. $100.00 – 125.00

Row 1: *Kliban Cat* Christmas mug, "Sigma the Tastesetter, designed by B. Kliban." Wooldridge. $35.00 – 45.00

Kliban Cat in Bathtub covered box, "Sigma the Tastesetter, designed by B. Kliban." Wooldridge. $300.00 – 325.00

Kliban Cat Playing Guitar candy jar, "Sigma the Tastesetter, designed by B. Kliban." Wooldridge. $75.00 – 100.00

Kliban Cat in Top Hat covered box, "Sigma the Tastesetter, designed by B. Kliban." Wooldridge. $60.00 – 75.00

Kliban Cat with Kiss covered container, "Sigma the Tastesetter, designed by B. Kliban." Wooldridge. $150.00 – 175.00

Kliban Cat covered sugar, "Sigma the Tastesetter, designed by B. Kliban." Wooldridge. $60.00 – 75.00

Kliban Cat creamer, "Sigma the Tastesetter, designed by B. Kliban." Wooldridge. $55.00 – 65.00

Kliban Cat Cowboy covered box, "Sigma the Tastesetter, designed by B. Kliban." Wooldridge. $150.00 – 175.00

Row 2: *Kliban Cat* bookends, "© Sigma © B. Kliban" incised. Paper label "Tastesetter © Sigma, PLEASE NOTE THAT ALL PIECES ARE HAND DECORATED, SO COLOR VARIANCE COULD OCCUR. LABORATORY TESTED TO COMPLY WITH FDA GUIDELINES, Made in Japan." $125.00 – 150.00

Below: *Kliban Cat* picture frame, "Sigma – B. Kliban." Darrow. $100.00 – 125.00

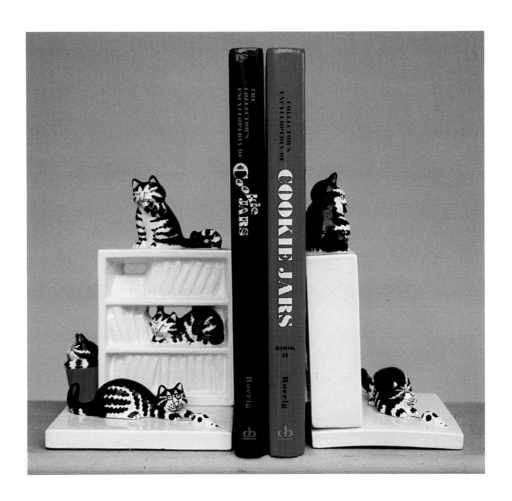

Row 1:   Sigma catalog sheet:

540 Kliban Cat and *Gramophone* music box. $225.00 – 275.00

246 Kliban Cat in Airplane teapot. $325.00 – 375.00

209 Kliban Cat face mug. $15.00 – 20.00

Row 2:   *555 Kliban Cat on Heart* covered box. $150.00 – 175.00

531 Kliban Cat soap dish. $140.00 – 160.00

Row 3:   Sigma catalog sheet:

224 Hatching Kliban Cat salt and pepper set. $200.00+

223 Kliban Cat and *Phonograph* salt and pepper set. $200.00+

Below: *Kliban Cat* wall plaque, "Sigma B. Kliban." Paper label "Japan." Signed
"B. Kliban" on front. Darrow. $70.00 – 90.00

Sigma catalog sheet:

A. *Miss Piggy* face mug.	$12.00 – 15.00
B. *Rowlf Playing Piano* covered box.	$275.00 – 325.00
C. *Miss Piggy* bank.	$25.00 – 35.00
D. *Kermit* and *Fozzie Bear* bookends.	$225.00 – 250.00
E. *Swedish Chef* cheese server.	$200.00 – 250.00
F. *Kermit* picture frame.	$150.00 – 175.00
G. *Kermit* and *Miss Piggy* salt and pepper set.	$100.00 – 125.00
H. *Kermit* face mug.	$12.00 – 15.00
J. *Fozzie Bear* face mug.	$25.00 – 30.00
K. *Kermit* covered box.	$150.00 – 175.00
L. *Miss Piggy* bud vase.	$40.00 – 60.00
M. *Rowlf* face mug.	$30.00 – 35.00
N. *Statler* and *Waldorf* bookends.	$250.00 – 300.00
P. *Gonzo* covered sugar.	$60.00 – 75.00
Q. *Miss Piggy* teapot.	$150.00 – 200.00
R. *Kermit* creamer.	$60.00 – 75.00
S. *Face Mugs,* set of 4 (Kermit, Miss Piggy, Fozzie, Rowlf).	$80.00 – 95.00
T. *Kermit* cookie jar.	$375.00 – 425.00
U. *Muppets* 3-piece canister set.	$650.00 – 750.00
Y. *Kermit* soap dish.	$100.00 – 125.00

The Muppets. Prime Time Entertainers.

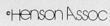

©Henson Assoc

20

Sigma catalog sheet:

Row 1: *531 Miss Piggy* heart-shaped soap dish. $100.00 – 125.00

Row 2: *313 Dr. Teeth* face mug. $50.00 – 60.00

312 Gonzo face mug. $60.00 – 75.00

311 Animal face mug. $75.00 – 85.00

Below: Sigma catalog sheet:

620 Miss Piggy candle holder. $100.00 – 125.00

2735277531

313

312

311

2735277

Row 1:	Sigma catalog sheet:	
	223 Swedish Chef and *Pepper Grinder* salt and pepper set.	$175.00 – 200.00
	230 set of 4 egg cups.	
	Floyd.	$50.00 – 75.00
	Waldorf.	$50.00 – 75.00
	Sam (the eagle).	$50.00 – 75.00
	Statler.	$50.00 – 75.00
	253 Kermit and *Miss Piggy Gondola* relish.	$200.00 – 225.00
Below:	*Miss Piggy on Shell*, chip and dip.	$225.00 – 250.00

Row 1:   Sigma catalog sheet:

        114 McGruff child's set (mug bowl, plate). $30.00 – 40.00

        650 McGruff bank. $75.00 – 95.00

        610 McGruff picture frame. $30.00 – 40.00

Row 2:   Sigma catalog sheet:

        300 McGruff mug. $12.00 – 15.00

        239 McGruff cookie jar. $325.00 – 375.00

        760 McGruff tumbler. $8.00 – 10.00

Below: *781 McGruff* light switch plate. $8.00 – 10.00

        805 McGruff key keeper. $12.00 – 15.00

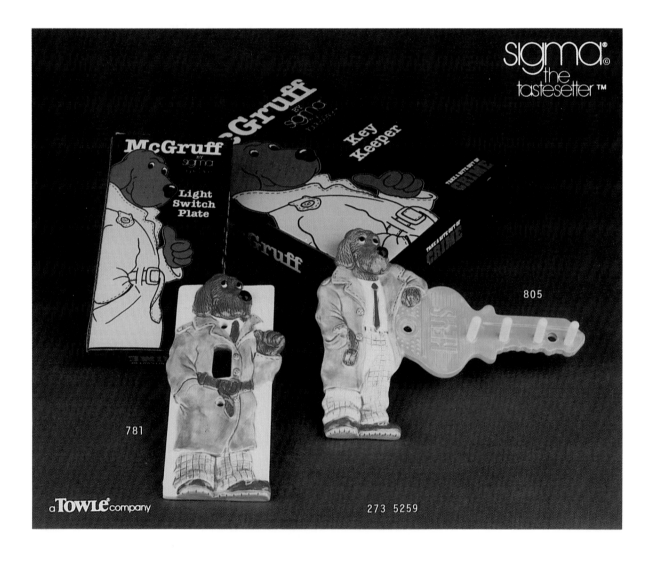

Row 1: Sigma catalog sheet:

501 Yoda vase. $70.00 – 80.00

651 Yoda bank. $50.00 – 60.00

223 Yoda salt and pepper set. $200.00+

239 Star Wars cookie jar. $125.00 – 150.00

224 R2-D2 and *R5-D4* salt and pepper set. $200.00+

Row 2: *540 C-3PO* music box. $200.00+

801 C-3PO pencil tray. $30.00 – 40.00

301 Luke Skywalker (X-Wing Fighter Pilot) face mug. $40.00 – 60.00

245 Tauntaun teapot. $200.00+

Below: Sigma catalog sheet:

Darth Vader/Chewbacca bookends. $200.00+

Row 1: Sigma catalog sheet:

620 Yoda candle holder. $200.00+

535 Yoda candy jar. $200.00+

760 Yoda pencil holder. $100.00 – 125.00

Row 2: *759 Rebel Snowspeeder* toothbrush holder. $75.00 – 85.00

758 Landspeeder soap dish. $40.00 – 60.00

Below: Sigma catalog sheet:

Row 1: *312 Lando Calrissian* (Skiff Guard disguise) face mug. $60.00 – 75.00

308 Klaatu face mug. $25.00 – 35.00

309 Imperial Biker Scout face mug. $60.00 – 75.00

541 Sy Snoodles/Max Rebo Band music box. $250.00+

Row 2: *652 Jabba the Hutt* bank. $75.00 – 85.00

310 Gamorrean Guard face mug. $25.00 – 35.00

311 Wicket W. Warrick face mug. $25.00 – 35.00

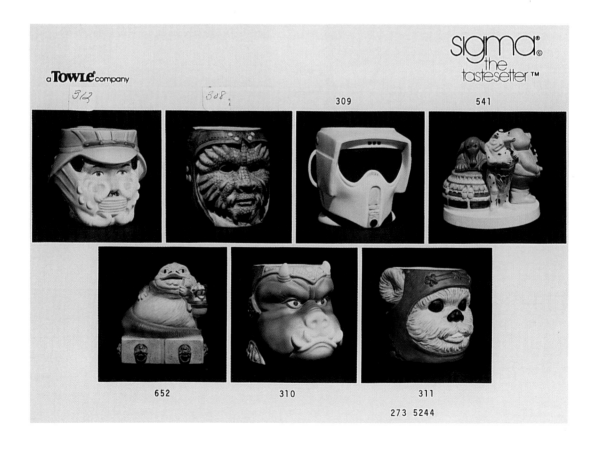

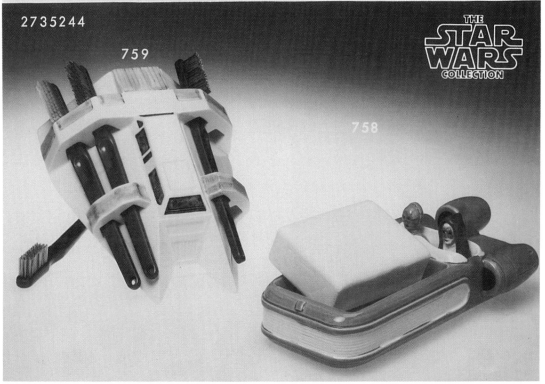

STAR JARS

Peter A. Gemmi, founded Star Jars, Inc., Palm Beach, Florida, in 1994. Star Jars is a designer/distributor of licensed, limited edition collectibles.

Row 1: *Dorothy & Toto,* "Star Jars™ Limited Edition 006 Dorothy & Toto U.S.A. Treasure Craft WIZARD OF OZ ©1994 Turner Entertainment ___of 1939." $325.00 – 375.00

Cowardly Lion, "Star Jars™ Limited Edition 001 Cowardly Lion U.S.A. Treasure Craft WIZARD OF OZ™ ©1994 Turner Entertainment ___of 1939." $250.00 – 300.00

Row 2: *Scarecrow,* "Star Jars™ Limited Edition 003 Scarecrow U.S.A. Treasure Craft WIZARD OF OZ™ ©1994 Turner Entertainment ___of 1939." $250.00 – 300.00

Tin Man, "Star Jars™ Limited Edition 002 Tin man U.S.A. Treasure Craft WIZARD OF OZ™ ©1994 Turner Entertainment ___of 1939." $250.00 – 300.00

Row 3: *Wicked Witch,* "Star Jars™ Limited Edition 004 Wicked Witch U.S.A. Treasure Craft WIZARD OF OZ™ ©1994 Turner Entertainment ___of 1939." $325.00 – 375.00

Glinda, "Star Jars™ Limited Edition 005 Glinda U.S.A. Treasure Craft WIZARD OF OZ™ ©1994 Turner Entertainment ___of 1939." $250.00 – 300.00

Below: *Ruby Slippers,* model of production sample (hopefully, final phase for remaining 546 pieces). $725.00 – 775.00

Ozware, cookie jar, clay sculpted with characters in relief along yellow brick road. Issue price $44.00

Row 1: *Winged Monkey,* 13⅝" high, "Star Jars™ Limited Edition 010 Winged Monkey U.S.A. Treasure Craft WIZARD OF OZ™ ©1994 Turner Entertainment ___of 1939." $325.00 – 375.00

Munchkin Mayor, 13½" high, "Star Jars™ Limited Edition 009 Munchkin Mayor U.S.A. Treasure Craft WIZARD OF OZ™ ©1994 Turner Entertainment ___of 1939." $325.00 – 375.00

Row 2: *Wizard of Oz,* 14½" high, "Star Jars™ Limited Edition 007 Wizard U.S.A. Treasure Craft WIZARD OF OZ ©1994 Turner Entertainment ___of 1939." $325.00 – 375.00

Professor Marvel 14½" high, "Star Jars™ Limited Edition 007 Wizard U.S.A. Treasure Craft WIZARD OF OZ ©1994 Turner Entertainment ___of 1939." $325.00 – 375.00

Row 3: *Emerald City* (front/back) 15½" high, "011 EMERALD CITY Star Jars™ Limited Edition Treasure Craft WIZARD OF OZ © 1996 Turner Entertainment ___of 625." $500.00 – 600.00

Below: *Ruby Slippers,* prototypes with "THERE'S NO PLACE LIKE HOME." embossed on front. Davis.   Value not determined

Ruby Slippers, original pie-shaped design, plagued with production problems 79 pieces of the original 625 were successfully produced). The embossed inscription featured on prototypes was replaced with gold decal. $1,500.00+

Row 1:   *Betty Boop* (as Juliet), cookie jar prototype. $250.00 – 275.00

King Kong, "012 KING KONG Star JARS LIMITED EDITIONS Treasure Craft A PFALTZGRAFF CO. KING KONG © 1996 TURNER ENTERTAINMENT ___ OF 500." Stamped on dry foot "MEXICO." $250.00 – 275.00

Row 2:   *Mammy/Pappy Yokum,* "025 Mammy & Pappy Yokum Star JARS Limited Editions ___ of 750 CHINA Treasure Craft A PFALTZGRAFF COMPANY © 1997 Capp Enterprise, Inc. All rights reserved." $225.00 – 275.00

Casper stacking salt and pepper set from *Casper the Movie,* "Casper © 1995 U.C.S. and Amblin. ™Harvey, STAR JARS, Made in China," bottom of train and "© 1995 U.C.S. and Amblin" rim of Casper shaker. $35.00 – 40.00

Row 3:   *Bozo,* 50TH Anniversary. "Star Jars LIMITED EDITIONS 013 ___ OF 750 BOZO 50TH Treasure Craft A PFALTZGRAFF COMPANY BOZO © 1995 Larry Harmon Picture Corp. 'Bozo'™ & © Larry Harmon Pictures Corp. Hollywood CA 90028." $225.00 – 275.00

Bozo stacking salt and pepper set, "Bozo ™ & © 1996 Larry Harmon Pictures Corp. Hollywood CA 90028 Star Jars, Made in China" on bottom of car. "© 1996 LHPC" on Bozo. $35.00 – 40.00

Below: *Herman Munster,* "Star Jars LIMITED EDITIONS, 017 ___ of 750, Treasure Craft A PFALTZGRAFF COMPANY, HERMAN MUNSTER THE MUNSTERS © 1996 KAYRO VUE PRODUCTIONS. ™UNIVERSAL STUDIOS, INC." $225.00 – 275.00

Grandpa Munster, "Star Jars LIMITED EDITIONS, 016 ___ of 750, Treasure Craft A PFALTZGRAFF COMPANY, GRANDPA MUNSTER THE MUNSTERS © 1996 KAYRO VUE PRODUCTIONS. ™UNIVERSAL STUDIOS, INC." $225.00 – 275.00

251

Row 1:   Star Wars:

                Hans Solo clay sculpture. $250.00 – 275.00

                Luke Skywalker clay scupture. $250.00 – 275.00

Row 2:   *C-3PO* clay sculpture. $250.00 – 275.00

Below: *Obi-Wan (Ben) Kenobi* prototype. $250.00 – 275.00

                Obi-Wan (Ben) Kenobi. $250.00 – 275.00

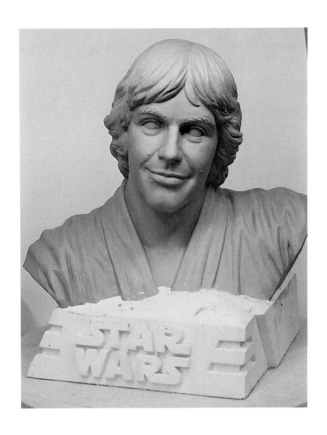

Row 1:	*Wicket W. Warrick* (Ewok) clay sculpture.	$250.00 – 275.00
	Gamorrean Guard clay sculpture.	$250.00 – 275.00
Row 2:	*Jabba the Hutt* clay sculpture.	$250.00 – 275.00
Below:	*Chewbacca* prototype.	$250.00 – 275.00
	Chewbacca.	$250.00 – 275.00

TREASURE CRAFT

In 1996 Treasure Craft made the transition from being a manufacturing-focused company to a design, marketing, and sales company.

Row 1: *Balloon,* "Treasure Craft © Made in USA" on inside lid. Snyder. — $30.00 – 40.00

Bear, "Treasure Craft © Made in USA" on inside lid. "Treasure Craft © USA" on base. Snyder. — $30.00 – 40.00

Potbellied Stove, "Treasure Craft © Made in USA" on inside lid. Paper label inside base, "Treasure Craft © USA." Snyder. — $30.00 – 40.00

Row 2: *Puppy,* "Treasure Craft © Made in USA" on inside lid. Snyder. — $30.00 – 40.00

Seymour J. Snailsworth (Rose-Petal Place™), "Treasure Craft © Made in USA" on inside lid. "©1983 David Kirschner Productions. All rights reserved." — $375.00 – 425.00

Engine, "Treasure Craft © USA" inside lid. Paper label inside base. Snyder. — $35.00 – 45.00

Row 3: *Hobby Horse,* "Treasure Craft © USA" inside lid. Snyder. — $40.00 – 50.00

Elephant, "Treasure Craft © USA" inside lid. "Treasure Craft © USA," base. Snyder. — $30.00 – 40.00

Hobby Horse, "Treasure Craft © USA" inside lid. Snyder. — $45.00 – 55.00

Below: *Tumbles the Hedgehog* (Rose-Petal Place™), a happy-go-lucky fellow, always full of fun and laughs. — $425.00 – 475.00

Elmer (Rose-Petal Place™), the elm tree knows everything about Rose-Petal Place™ because he records everything in his diary. — $800.00+

Seymour J. Snailsworth (Rose-Petal Place™), a snail of great wisdom. He carries his home on his back, and can always be called upon for a word or two of advice. — $375.00 – 425.00

256

Row 1:   *Golf Ball*, "Treasure Craft © Made in USA." $45.00 – 50.00

                Football, "Treasure Craft © Made in USA." $45.00 – 50.00

                Baseball, "Treasure Craft © Made in USA." $35.00 – 40.00

Row 2:   *Soccer Ball*, "Treasure Craft © Made in USA." $40.00 – 45.00

                Baseball Boy, "Treasure Craft © Made in USA" incised on back. $40.00 – 50.00

                Bowling Ball, "Treasure Craft © Made in USA." $40.00 – 45.00

Row 3:   *Basketball*, "Treasure Craft © Made in USA." $35.00 – 40.00

                Eightball, "Treasure Craft © Made in USA." $70.00 – 80.00

                Tennis Ball, "Treasure Craft © Made in USA." $35.00 – 40.00

Below: *Pirate Bust*, "Treasure Craft © Made in USA." Blumenfeld. $275.00 – 325.00

                Bunny "©Treasure Craft," rim of lid. Candee. $50.00 – 60.00

TWIN WINTON

For additional, extensive coverage of Twin Winton Ceramics, see *Cookie Jars, Book I* and *II* by Roerig.

Row 1:   *Cop bank,* gray. "Twin Winton © CA USA." Whetstine. $50.00 – 60.00

               Dutch Girl napkin holder, gray, "Twin Winton © San Juan Capistrano Calif." Whetstine. $45.00 – 55.00

Row 2:   *Happy Bull,* gray, initials "V S" etched into clay. $70.00 – 90.00

               Cow, gray, unmarked. $70.00 – 90.00

Below: Display plaque in gray. Unusual, extremely hard to find. Eggert/Seman. $275.00 – 325.00

The following two pages show all 18 Collector's Series jars.

Row 1:   *Rabbit,* incised "TWIN WINTON © CALIF. USA."
Stamped, "TWIN WINTON © SAN JUAN CAPISTRANO CALIF.
USA." Artist initials, "RH." $175.00 – 225.00

Cookie Elf, "TWIN WINTON COLLECTOR'S SERIES California, U.S.A."
Signed "MAC." $200.00 – 250.00.

Pirate Fox, "Twin Winton, Made in Calif. USA © 63" incised into
pottery. Stamped, "Twin Winton © San Juan Capistrano, Calif.
U.S.A." $150.00 – 175.00

Row 2:   *Elephant,* unmarked. $100.00 – 125.00

Hobby Horse, "Twin Winton Collector's Series." $250.00 – 275.00

Owl, stamped, "Twin Winton Collector's Series © California USA."
Incised into pottery, "Twin Winton © Calif. USA." $100.00 – 125.00

Row 3:   *Police* (Bear), "Twin Winton Collector's Series © California USA." $100.00 – 125.00

Policeman (Cop), "Twin Winton Calif. USA." $150.00 – 175.00

Bear (Ranger), "Twin Winton © San Juan Capistrano, Calif. USA."
Artist initials, "J.L." $100.00 – 125.00

Below: *Shaggy Pup* (Dog with Bow), Collector's Series, unmarked. Rare. $275.00 – 325.00

Row 1:   *Donkey,* Collector's Series, "Twin Winton © Calif. USA" incised into
pottery. Stamped "Twin Winton Collector's Series © California USA." $175.00 – 200.00

Barn, Collector's Series, "Twin Winton © San Juan Capistrano Calif.
USA." $100.00 – 125.00

Rooster, Collector's Series, "Twin Winton Collector's Series © California
USA." $150.00 – 175.00

Row 2:   *Mopsey* (Raggedy Ann), Collector's Series, "San Juan Capistrano
Calif. USA." $125.00 – 150.00

Goose, "1961 © Twin Winton, Made in Calif." incised into pottery.
Stamped "Twin Winton Collector's Series © California USA." $200.00 – 225.00

Flopsey (Raggedy Andy), Collector's Series, "Twin Winton San Juan
Capistrano Calif. USA." $125.00 – 150.00

Row 3:   *Dutch Girl,* incised "TWIN WINTON © CALIF. U.S.A." Stamped,
TWIN WINTON © SAN JUAN CAPISTRANO CALIF. USA." Darrow. $150.00 – 175.00

Mouse, Collector's Series, unmarked. Darrow. $100.00 – 125.00

Little Lamb, Collector's Series, "Twin Winton Collector's Series
© California USA." Artist initials, "P/S." Darrow. $100.00 – 125.00

Below: *Foo Dog* salt and pepper shakers with factory-set rhinestones,
"TWIN WINTON CALIF. U.S.A." Rare!   Price not determined.

Row 1: *Pirate Fox* bank, "TWIN WINTON CALIF. U.S.A." $60.00 – 70.00

Nut bank, "TWIN WINTON © CALIF. U.S.A." $55.00 – 65.00

Big Boy bank, "W." $325.00 – 375.00

Row 2: *Church.* $275.00 – 325.00

Lion and Lamb, "Witness Pottery 3001 RED HILL RD. 1-105 COSTA MESA, CALIFORNIA," part of a Christian pottery line made by Twin Winton for Witness Pottery of Santa Ana. Don Winton was in partnership with Jim Willems of Witness Pottery in 1972. All the Witness Pottery line was glazed with the exception of the Lion and Lamb cookie jar. Rare. $275.00 – 325.00

Row 3: *Apple* salt or pepper shaker, "TWIN WINTON."   Set $80.00 – 90.00

Pear cookie jar in pineapple color, unmarked. $125.00 – 90.00

Apple salt or pepper shaker, "TWIN WINTON."   Set $80.00 – 90.00

Below: *Pear* cookie jar in wood finish, unmarked. Darrow. $100.00 – 125.00

Pear cookie jar in pineapple, unmarked. Darrow. $125.00 – 150.00

Pear cookie jar in avocado, unmarked. Darrow. $70.00 – 90.00

Pear cookie jar in orange, unmarked. Darrow. $70.00 – 90.00

Row 2: *Apple* cookie jar in wood finish, unmarked. Darrow. $100.00 – 125.00

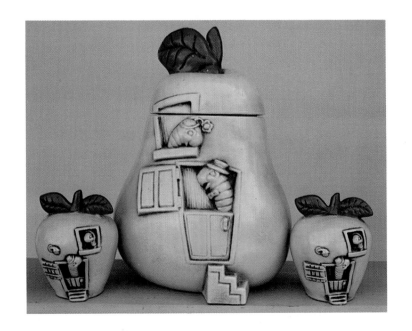

Back stamp used on base of
the *Lion and Lamb* cookie jar.

Row 1:   *Mountain Woman* salt or pepper shaker, unmarked.   Set $20.00 – 25.00

Mountain Man keeper incised "Twin Winton © KS Made in USA." $75.00 – 85.00

Mountain Man salt or pepper shaker, unmarked.   Set $20.00 – 25.00

Row 2:   *Tumbler,* trimmed with fired-on gold. "Twin Winton Pasadena, Cal." $25.00 – 35.00

Steak Plate, "Twin Winton — Steak Plate Pasadena California." $70.00 – 80.00

Cowboy handle mugs, "K Open Range TW Twin Winton Pasadena." $30.00 – 35.00

Row 3:   *Cat & Fiddle* accent lamp "Twin Winton ©USA." Candee. $175.00 – 200.00

Friar Tuck honey container, 6" high "© TWIN WINTON Calif USA." Whetstine. $85.00+

Below: *Shack* talking picture. $75.00 – 95.00

Shack bank. $50.00 – 60.00

Row 1:   *Elf* napkin holder, unmarked. $40.00 – 50.00

                  Rabbit cocktail napkin holder, unmarked. $100.00 – 125.00

                  Owl napkin holder, unmarked. $45.00 – 55.00

Row 2:   *Teddy Bear,* unmarked, probably had foil label at one time. $45.00 – 55.00

                  Cow, gold-colored rectangular label on bottom of base, "BEAUTIFUL HAND CRAFTED CERAMICS MADE IN U.S.A. SAN JUAN CAPISTRANO, CA 92675" surrounding "TWIN WINTON CALIFORNIA" in center. $60.00 – 75.00

                  Bear (Ranger), gold-colored rectangular label on bottom of base, "BEAUTIFUL HAND CRAFTED CERAMICS MADE IN U.S.A. SAN JUAN CAPISTRANO, CA 92675" surrounding "TWIN WINTON CALIFORNIA" in center. $35.00 – 45.00

Row 3:   *Kitten* mug, unmarked. Whetstine. $30.00 – 40.00

                  Lamb mug, unmarked. Whetstine. $30.00 – 40.00

Row 4:   *Bear* mug, 3¼" high, unmarked. $30.00 – 40.00

                  Puppy mug, 3¼" high, unmarked. $30.00 – 40.00

Below: *Friar Tuck* pitcher (cruet?), done by man who bought Twin Winton from Bruce Winton. The pitcher appears to be an altered coin bank. "© TWIN WINTON Calif USA." $75.00 – 85.00

                  Friar Tuck bank, "© TWIN WINTON Calif USA." $50.00 – 60.00

                  Friar Tuck bank, "© TWIN WINTON Calif USA." $80.00 – 90.00

Row 1: *Rooster* napkin holder, unmarked. $45.00 – 55.00

Hen covered sugar, 4" high x 5" long, unmarked. Whetstine. $30.00 – 40.00

Rooster creamer, 5½" high x 7" long, unmarked. $25.00 – 35.00

Row 2: *Happy Bull* bank, "TWIN WINTON CALIF U.S.A." $55.00 – 65.00

Cow spoon rest, "Twin Winton © San Juan Capistrano Calif." $100.00 – 125.00

Row 3: *Squirrel* spoon rest, unmarked. $30.00 – 35.00

Lamb wall pocket, unmarked. $50.00 – 60.00

Poodle spoon rest, "©Twin Winton San Juan Capistrano Calif." $35.00 – 45.00

Below: *Raccoon* figurine, 5¾" high, "WINTON #115." $25.00 – 35.00

Raccoon figurine, 3¾" high, "WINTON #132." $15.00 – 20.00

Bear talking picture, unmarked. $100.00 – 125.00

Duck figurine, 2" high, "WINTON #59." $15.00 – 20.00

Mushroom figurine, 3" high, "WINTON 53." $20.00 – 25.00

Squirrel napkin holder, unmarked. $45.00 – 55.00

273

Row 1:   *Rabbit and Hatbox* planter, 5" high, stamped under glaze "TWIN WINTON © CERAMICS PASADENA, CALIF." $35.00 – 45.00

Rabbit and Wheelbarrow planter, 3½" high stamped under glaze "TWIN WINTON © CERAMICS PASADENA, CALIF." $35.00 – 45.00

Rabbit planter, 3½" high, incised "THE HAPPY LAND LINE, TWIN WINTON PASADENA CALIF." Stamped under glaze "TWIN WINTON © CERAMICS PASADENA, CALIF." Whetstine. $35.00 – 45.00

Row 2:   *Humpty Dumpty* planter, "TWIN WINTON PASADENA CALIF." Potter. $45.00 – 55.00

Pan, from Greek mythology, playing panpipe, 5⅞" high, unmarked. $100.00 – 125.00

Row 3:   *Rag Doll,* 9¼" high, unmarked. Chapman. $375.00+

Santa candy container or planter, 6½" high, "TWIN WINTON CERAMICS © PASADENA CA." $100.00 – 125.00

Below: *Tommy Turtle* salt or pepper, "D." Whetstine.   Set $100.00 – 125.00

Gnome stump planter, "W." $35.00 – 45.00

Elephant planter, stamped under glaze "TWIN WINTON © CERAMICS PASADENA, CALIF." $40.00 – 50.00

Tommy Turtle cookie jar, unmarked, verified by Don Winton. $325.00 – 375.00

Duck figurine, "TWIN WINTON CA USA." $15.00 – 20.00

Row 1: *Little Girl* and *Elephant* figurine, 3½" high, "Twinton © 1972 T-14." Whetstine. $45.00 – 55.00

Mouseketeer w/lollipop, Twinton figurine. Posner. $100.00 – 125.00

Mousketeer w/airplane, Twinton figurine. Posner. $100.00 – 125.00

Row 2: *Oriental Boy* figurine, "Twinton © 1972 T-15." $40.00 – 50.00

Oriental Girl figurine, "Twinton © 1972 T-16." $40.00 – 45.00

Bambi planter, "TWIN WINTON © CALIF USA." Whetstine. $35.00 – 45.00

Row 3: *Cable Car* salt and pepper set, unmarked. $75.00 – 85.00

Below: *Boxing Kangaroo,* unmarked, verified by Don Winton. Davis. $500.00+

Boxing Kangaroo, unmarked, verified by Don Winton. Rhinehimer. $500.00+

Base of Boxing Kangaroo signed by Don Winton at the Third Annual National Cookie Jar Show.

Row 1:   *Bear* (Ranger) cookie jar. Darrow. $40.00 – 50.00

                   Cookie Elf. Darrow. $50.00 – 60.00

                   Tugboat cookie jar, without smoke. Unmarked Hull. $175.00 – 225.00

Row 2:   *Trolley Car* dime bank. Darrow. $65.00 – 75.00

                   Poodle napkin holder, unmarked. Darrow. $45.00 – 55.00

Row 3:   *Volkswagen* bank, incised "TWIN WINTON © SAN JUAN CAPISTRANO, CA." Stamped, "TWIN WINTON © San Juan Capistrano, Calif. U. S. A." Perez. $100.00 – 125.00

UNGEMACH

Additional Ungemach cookie jars are featured in *Cookie Jars, Book I.* A short history and explanation of the company can be found in *Book II.* In addition to the cookie jars now properly identified, Ungemach did contract work for Walt Disney, distributed through Leeds.

Below: *Happy Clown,* 10½" high, "USA" on back. $575.00 – 625.00

               Schoolhouse," 11" high, "CJ 7 USA. $125.00 – 150.00

WADE

Wade porcelain and pottery products have long been a documented collectible. What captured our interest was the advertising pieces produced by Wade, Burslem, England, for Lyons Tetley. Being cookie jar and go-with addicts, it was natural to gather the Tetley items, then Harrods Door Man, and now we have to have (at least) the International Association of Jim Beam Bottle and Specialities Clubs cookie jars.

Row 1: *Brew Gaffer* teapot, 5¼" high, "AN ORIGINAL DESIGN FOR TETLEY GB BY WADE ENGLAND. ©Tetley GB Limited 1996." $75.00 – 85.00

Brew Gaffer cookie jar, 8⅜" high, "AN ORIGINAL DESIGN FOR LYONS TETLEY BY WADE ENGLAND." $125.00 – 150.00

Brew Gaffer and Sidney teapot (front side), "AN ORIGINAL DESIGN FOR LYONS TETLEY BY WADE ENGLAND." $75.00 – 85.00

Row 2: *Brew Gaffer and Sidney* teapot (back side), 5" high, "AN ORIGINAL DESIGN FOR LYONS TETLEY BY WADE ENGLAND." $75.00 – 80.00

Sidney and Brew Gaffer (Teafolk) salt and pepper set. Current, Oct 1996 –.... Set $50.00 – 60.00

Row 3: *Brew Gaffer* money box (bank), 5¾" high, "AN ORIGINAL DESIGN FOR TETLEY GB BY WADE ENGLAND. ©Tetley GB Limited 1996." $75.00 – 85.00

Delivery Truck tea canister (cookie jar) 5¼" high, 9" long, "AN ORIGINAL DESIGN FOR LYONS TETLEY BY WADE ENGLAND." $200.00 – 225.00

Brew Gaffer money box (bank), 5¼" high, "Made exclusively for LYONS TETLEY by WADE." Used as a promotional item from September 1989 through the end of July 1990 by Lyons Tetley. Three proofs of purchases required. $100.00 – 125.00

Below: *Sidney and Brew Gaffer* (Teafolk) salt and pepper set. Retired 1990 – 1992. Tompkins. Set $110.00 – 125.00

Row 1: *Peasant* cookie jar, 10½" high, made for Boots Drug Store, 1991, by Wade. Devilbliss. $90.00 – 110.00

Peasant teapot, 6½" high, "WADE ENGLAND." Devilbliss. $75.00 85.00

Row 2: *Wade/Ellis* cookie jar, fox finial, designed by cartoonist Dick Ellis for the International Association of Jim Bean Bottle and Specialties Clubs. Wade Ceramics filled the void for Jim Bean collectors since the closure of Regal China. $65.00 – 75.00

Wade/Ellis cookie jar, fox finial, designed by cartoonist Dick Ellis for the International Association of Jim Bean Bottle and Specialties Clubs. $65.00 – 70.00

Below: *Harrods Door Man* salt or pepper shaker, "*Harrods* KNIGHTSBRIDGE." Set $75.00 – 85.00

Harrods Door Man cookie jar, "*Harrods* KNIGHTSBRIDGE." $125.00 – 175.00

Harrods Door Man salt or pepper shaker, "*Harrods* KNIGHTSBRIDGE 15." Set $75.00 – 85.00

WALT DISNEY

Row 1: Treasure Craft Catalog photograph featuring Homegrown Mickey.

Canister set, 4-piece, 8" – 10" high. — Issue price $70.00 – 75.00

Mickey & Barrel cookie jar, 12" high. — Issue price $50.00 – 55.00

Mickey/Wheelbarrow salt and pepper set, 5" high. — Issue price $25.00 – 30.00

Mixing Bowl Set, 3-piece, 6", 8", 10" dia. — 3-piece set $50.00

Pitcher, 9" high, 88 oz. — Issue price $20.00 – 25.00

Mickey & Carrots cookie jar, 12" high. — Issue price $50.00 – 55.00

Mickey/Minnie mug set, 14 oz. — Issue price $20.00 – 25.00

Row 2: *Mickey* and *Minnie Santa* salt and pepper set, "©DISNEY" incised. On transparent paper label, "MICKEY & CO. © DISNEY LICENSEE ENESCO MADE IN CHINA." — Issue price $19.00

Mickey Santa cookie jar, "©DISNEY" incised. On transparent paper label, "MICKEY & CO. © DISNEY LICENSEE ENESCO MADE IN CHINA." — Issue price $70.00

Minnie and *Mickey Santa* banks, "©DISNEY" incised. On transparent paper label, "MICKEY & CO. © DISNEY LICENSEE ENESCO MADE IN CHINA." — Issue price each $15.00

Row 3: *Minnie* decorating tree bank, incised "©DISNEY." On transparent paper label, "MICKEY & CO. © DISNEY LICENSEE ENESCO MADE IN CHINA." Discontinued. — $30.00 – 40.00

Mickey and Friends decorating tree, "© DISNEY MADE IN TAIWAN." Paper label, "HAND-CRAFTED IN TAIWAN." Disney store exclusive. — $175.00 – 225.00

Donald and Toy Sack bank, incised "©DISNEY." On transparent paper label, "MICKEY & CO. © DISNEY LICENSEE ENESCO MADE IN CHINA." Discontinued. — $30.00 – 40.00

Below: *Mickey Mouse,* single not turnabout. "MICKEY MOUSE ©WALT DISNEY USA." Distributed by Leeds. Jessen. — Price not determined.

284

Row 1:   *Meeko* (Lion King), "© DISNEY TREASURE CRAFT." Stamped, "MEXICO" on unglazed rim of lid. Discontinued. $80.00 – 90.00

Pocahontas and John Smith (Pocahontas) polyvinyl chloride (PVC) bank, "© DISNEY CHINA." $8.00 – 10.00

Percy and Meeko (Pocahontas) salt and pepper set, "DANAWARES MONTREAL © Disney TAIWAN." $25.00 – 35.00

Row 2:   *Gargoyle* (Hugo, Victor, and Laverne) bank, high-impact plastic, "© DISNEY CE CHINA." $8.00 – 10.00

Laverne (gargoyle) toy, "MANUFACTURED FOR BURGER KING CORPORATION © DISNEY MADE IN CHINA KE-55." $0.90 – 1.10

Hugo, "© DISNEY TREASURE CRAFT." On dry foot (unglazed pottery rim), "MEXICO."   Issue price $50.00

Laverne and Victor salt and pepper set, "© DISNEY," Stamped on dry foot, "Mexico."   Issue price $25.00

Row 3:   *Abu* (Aladdin) ceramic bank, "DISNEY." Paper label "Schmid Malaysia." Robertson. $25.00 – 35.00

Genie cookie jar, full-bodied, "© Disney MEXICO" on bottom of base. Sold exclusively through Disney Theme Parks. $125.00 – 150.00

Genie and Magic Lamp stacking salt and pepper shakers, "©DISNEY TREASURE CRAFT USA." $28.00 – 32.00

Genie and Magic Lamp teapot, "©DISNEY TREASURE CRAFT MADE IN USA" on base, "©DISNEY T/C USA" on rim of lid. $40.00 – 50.00

Genie Bust cookie jar, ©DISNEY, small, gold-colored, rectangular label, "MADE IN THAILAND." Disney store exclusive. $150.00 – 175.00

Below: *Practical Pig* cookie jar, sculpted by Don Winton for Hagen-Renaker. Incised "© DISNEY." Stamped "Hagen-Renaker." Hamburg. $1,800.00+

Figaro cookie jar, Hagen-Renaker, "Walt Disney Productions." Rare. $2,200.00+

Row 1: *Simba* cookie jar (The Lion King), impressed around upper rim lid, "TREASURE CRAFT ©DISNEY." Disc. $75.00 – 95.00

Timon spoon rest (The Lion King), "©DISNEY TREASURE CRAFT USA." $15.00 – 20.00

Simba and Nala salt and pepper set (The Lion King), "©DISNEY T/C." $25.00 – 35.00

Simba trivet (The Lion King), "©DISNEY TREASURE CRAFT USA." $20.00 – 25.00

Row 2: *Dopey* cookie jar (Snow White and the Seven Dwarfs), "©DISNEY TREASURE CRAFT" around rim of lid.   Issue price $50.00

Snow White and Dopey salt and pepper shaker set (Snow White and the Seven Dwarfs). Snow White was incised and Dopey stamped, "©DISNEY CHINA."   Issue price $12.95

Snow White (Snow White and the Seven Dwarfs), ©DISNEY TREASURE CRAFT USA." The majority of the Snow White cookie jars were produced first in Mexico then China. Ours is a production sample made in the "USA."   Issue price $50.00

Row 3: *Mickey Mouse Club House,* from Leisuramics commercial ceramic mold. This accounts for the endless variety in decorating found. Marked, "©WALT DISNEY PROD." $125.00 – 175.00

Dopey cookie jar (Snow White and the Seven Dwarfs), "©DISNEY TREASURE CRAFT" around rim of lid.   Issue price $50.00

Below: *Sleepy trivet* (Snow White and the Seven Drawfs).   Issue price $17.00

Happy (Snow White and the Seven Dwarfs) utensil holder (w/utensils), "© DISNEY USA TREASURE CRAFT."   Issue price $25.00

Sneezy and Bashful salt and pepper set (Snow White and the Seven Dwarfs), "©DISNEY TREASURE CRAFT USA."   Issue price $20.00

Grumpy spoon rest (Snow White and the Seven Dwarfs), "©DISNEY TREASURE CRAFT USA."   Issue price $10.00

Row 1:   *Mufusa and Simba* ceramic bank, "© DISNEY MADE IN CHINA." $30.00 – 40.00

Pumba cookie jar, "Disney's THE LION KING © DISNEY Schmid. Words
by: Tim Rice Lyrics by: Elton John © 1994 WALT DISNEY, MUSIC
COMPANY/WONDERLAND MUSIC COMPANY, INC. ALL RIGHTS RESERVED."
Paper label, "HAKUNA MATATA Schmid SRI LANKA THIS MUSIC BOX
IS EQUIPPED WITH AN ON/OFF STOPPER DO NOT OVERWIND." $75.00 – 95.00

Goofy polyvinyl chloride (PVC) bank, "©DISNEY CHINA." Herndon
Roerig.   Issue price $6.00

Row 2:   *Dopey's Diamond* ceramic bank, "© Disney china."   Issue price $18.00

Snow White cylinder, "© DISNEY." Bottom of base, "CRAFTED
WITH PRIDE IN U.S.A. © Treasure Craft." $70.00 – 80.00

Toontown City Hall, "© DISNEY." Transparent label, "Mickey & Co.
© DISNEY LICENSEE ENESCO MADE IN CHINA."   Issue price $70.00

Below: *Dalmatians* (101 Dalmatians) polyvinyl chloride (PVC) bank,
"© DISNEY CHINA."   Issue price $6.00

Kanine Krunchies dog biscuit jar, "©DISNEY Made in Thailand."   Issue price $25.00

Danawares Corporation is a Canadian-based distributor.

Row 1:   *Donald Duck,* "© DISNEY DANAWARES TAIWAN." $100.00 – 125.00

     Goofy cookie jar, "© DISNEY DANAWARES TAIWAN." $100.00 – 125.00

Row 2:   *Mickey Mouse* cookie jar, "© DISNEY DANAWARES TAIWAN." $100.00 – 125.00

     Mickey/Minnie salt and pepper set, "© DISNEY DANAWARES TAIWAN." $20.00 – 25.00

     Minnie Mouse cookie jar, "© DISNEY DANAWARES TAIWAN." $100.00 – 125.00

Row 3:   *Mickey/Minnie* glass cylinder (Anchor Hocking), "© DISNEY" on decal. $20.00 – 25.00

     Mickey Mouse ceramic bank, "©DISNEY CHINA." Paper label, "Not intended for children under three (3) years of age. CAUTION: BANK IS CERAMIC AND BREAKABLE."   Issue price $18.00

     Mickey/Minnie floral cookie jar (4 qt.), "WOW" inside. "PFALTZGRAFF COPYRIGHT USA MICKEY & CO. ©Disney PFALTZGRAFF YORK, PA USA Since 1811."   Issue price $50.00

Below: *Mickey with Straw Hat,* "©DISNEY." Transparent label, "MICKEY & CO. LICENSEE ENESCO MADE IN CHINA."   Issue price $70.00

     Mickey with Top Hat, "©DISNEY MADE IN MALAYSIA" incised. "©DISNEY Licensed by Enesco Corporation Made in Malaysia." Gold-colored oval label, "ENESCO MADE IN MALAYSIA."   Issue price $70.00

Row 1:   *Chip-n-Dale* side of unmarked basket-handle biscuit jar. Martin.

If Disney $275.00 – 325.00

Donald Duck side of basket-handle biscuit jar, unmarked, Martin.

If Disney $275.00 – 325.00

Row 2:   *Mickey and Friends* canister, "Walt Disney Prod." Martin. $175.00 – 225.00

Mickey Toy Sack, "© DISNEY MEXICO." $95.00 – 125.00

Row 3:   *Disney Channel* cylinder "TREASURE CRAFT MADE IN USA" incised into lid. $125.00 – 150.00

Dalmatian ceramic bank, "DISNEY MADE IN TAIWAN." Paper label, "Not intended for children under three (3) years of age. CAUTION; BANK IS CERAMIC AND BREAKABLE."   Issue price $18.00

Dalmatians cylinder, "*Walt Disney's* 101 Dalmatians" on back. Embossed inside lid, "© TREASURE CRAFT." $55.00 – 65.00

Below: *Dumbo,* unmarked, 9⅝" high x 7¾" wide, one of four Disney jars produced at Metlox by Evan K. Shaw. Shaw's Disney license was issued to American Pottery in 1942. When American Pottery was destroyed by fire in 1946 the production of Disney products was temporarily halted until Shaw bought Metlox the same year.

    According to Carl Gibbs (*Collector's Encyclopedia of Metlox Potteries Identification and Values*), the foil label used to identify these pieces always reads "American Pottery Company" or "Evan K. Shaw Company" which were licensed concurrently by Disney to Shaw. Ochoa. $1,800.00+

Donald Duck, with American Pottery paper label produced at Metlox in 1949. A similar Donald was done later with Donald holding his hat rather than a cookie. Anderson. $3,000.00+

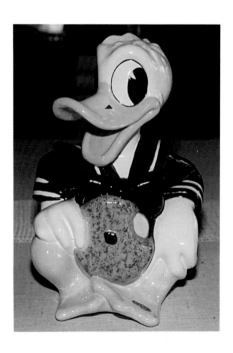

Row 1: *Goofy,* "Treasure Craft © Disney Mexico." Issue price $60.00

Donald Duck, "Treasure Craft © Disney Mexico." Issue price $60.00

Row 2: *School Bus,* 6" high x 10¼" long, "© 1961 Walt Disney Productions." Horelica. $425.00 – 475.00

Donald Duck teapot, "MADE IN ENGLAND." Grogan. $600.00+

Row 3: *Mickey Mouse* prototype, unmarked. The marked production version of this jar is featured in *Book I* on page 299. Interestingly enough, the catalog sheet on page 92, *Book II,* features both hands resting under Mickey's chin. Price not determined.

Below: *Donald and Pumpkin,* "Walt Disney Productions 805." Takasugi. $275.00 – 325.00

Mickey and Drum, "Walt Disney Productions #864." This jar is marked and Mickey's arm rests on the drum. Takasugi. $275.00 – 325.00

Row 1:   *Tigger* figurine, "©WALT DISNEY PROD JAPAN." Joy Roerig. $10.00 – 12.00

Winnie the Pooh and Eeyore stacking salt and pepper set, "©DISNEY
JAPAN." Joy Roerig. $28.00 – 32.00

Winnie the Pooh ceramic bank, "© Disney MADE IN CHINA." Paper label,
"Based on the 'Winnie the Pooh' works Copyright A.A. Milne and E.H.
Shepard." Joy Roerig.   Issue price $18.00

Tigger soakie, "HAND WASH ONLY © JOHNSON & JOHNSON CONSUMER
PRODUCTS, INC. 1996 DISNEY MATERIAL © DISNEY MADE IN CHINA
FOR AGES 6-48 MONTHS." Joy Roerig. $6.00 – 8.00

Row 2:   *Pluto Doghouse,* "GALLERY COLLECTION PLUTO by TREASURE CRAFT 1000
Piece Edition *Limited Edition* Made in the U.S.A. © DISNEY 1995." $275.00 – 325.00

Pluto Doghouse candy covered container, "A TELEFLORA GIFT FLOWERS
FROM MICKEY." Paper label, "MADE IN PHILIPPINES." $40.00-50.00

Row 3:   *Bambi,* unmarked. $800.00

Buzz Lightyear (Toy Story) telephone, paper label, "Buzz Lightyear
Phone Buzz9609 Complies with Part 68, FCC rules FCC Reg. Number
5UFCHN-24055-TE-E REN 0.9B LN16 Custom Manufactured in
China for Lenbrook Industries AOJL connector RJ11C." Paper label,
"Industry Canada 152 7555 A." Embossed, "Disney's Toy Story
Brooktel © Disney." $125.00 – 150.00

Buzz Lightyear, "LIMITED EDITION Production of this cookie jar was limited
to 1500 units. This is number: 391 GALLERY COLLECTION Disney's
TOY STORY Limited Edition Buzz Lightyear Cookie Jar by Treasure Craft
A PFALTZGRAFF COMPANY Made in China © Disney."   Issue price $300.00

Right: *Buzz Lightyear/Woody (Toy
Story)* salt and pepper set
by Treasure Craft. "© Disney
Treasure Craft."
              Issue price $30.00

Row 1: *Eeyore* (Holiday) covered sugar, "© DISNEY MADE IN CHINA."

2-piece set $40.00 – 50.00

Tigger's "HIDDEN TREASURE" bank. Part of Holiday Pooh line
released for Christmas 1994, "©DISNEY." Approximately 7½" high. $35.00 – 45.00

Holiday Pooh creamer, "©DISNEY MADE IN CHINA."   2-piece set $40.00 – 50.00

Row 2: *Winnie the Pooh/Tigger* salt and pepper set, "© DISNEY CHINA." $60.00 – 70.00

Holiday Treehouse cookie jar, "Made in, © DISNEY, China" on
impressed oval (three lines), approximately 11" high. $225.00 – 275.00

Row 3: *Holiday* teapot, "©DISNEY MADE IN CHINA." $75.00 – 95.00

Below: *Holiday Platter,* "©DISNEY MADE IN CHINA." $40.00 – 50.00

Holiday Mug Tree (pressed wood), "©Disney China" with four
ceramic mugs.   5-piece set, $50.00 – 60.00

Row 1: *Classic Pooh* trivet, "© DISNEY TREASURE CRAFT USA."   Issue price $20.00

"HUNNY" pot, "©DISNEY TREASURE CRAFT USA."   Issue price $25.00

Piglet/Pooh salt and pepper set, "©DISNEY T/C."   Issue price $25.00

Classic Pooh cookie jar distributed by Treasure Craft, "©DISNEY" on rim of lid.   Issue price $60.00

Row 2: *Winnie the Pooh* reading "ALL ABOUT HONEY" bank. Marked with transparent label with brown lettering and image of Pooh, "Classic POOH, ©DISNEY, DESIGNED BY CHARPENTE, TAIWAN." Approximately 5¾" high. $20.00 – 25.00

Winnie the Pooh and "Hunny" Pots bank, transparent label with brown lettering and image of Pooh, "Classic POOH, ©DISNEY, DESIGNED BY CHARPENTE, TAIWAN." Approximately 9¾" high. $40.00 – 50.00

Winnie the Pooh and honey pot bank, small. Marked with transparent label with brown lettering and image of Pooh, "Classic POOH, ©DISNEY, DESIGNED BY CHARPENTE, TAIWAN." Approximately 5½" high. $18.00 – 22.00

Row 3: *Winnie the Pooh Treehouse* (two sides), incised "©DISNEY DANAWARE THAILAND," on transparent label, $75.00 – 95.00

"FRIENDSHIP
Winnie the Pooh Cookie Jar

Tiggers don't like honey
But Eeyore needs the pot,
To help our hero Pooh Bear
Save Piglet from a spot."

Below: *Winnie the Pooh and friends* tree stump bank. "A VERY USEFUL THING TO KEEP BITS AND PIECES IN FOR TODAY OR TOMORROW." Marked with transparent label with brown lettering and image of Pooh, "Classic POOH, ©DISNEY, DESIGNED BY CHARPENTE, TAIWAN." Approximately 2¾" high. $30.00 – 35.00

WARNER BROTHERS

Row 1:   *The Brain* figurine, "MADE IN THAILAND TM & ©WB 94." $25.00 – 28.00

        The Brain and Pinky salt and pepper set, "MADE IN THAILAND."   Set $32.00 – 38.00

        Pinky figurine, "MADE IN THAILAND TM & ©WB 94." $25.00 – 28.00

Row 2:   *Pinky and The Brain* ceramic bank, 6" diameter, "TM © 96 WB MADE IN CHINA." The box is almost as great as the bank, "Hello. May I be the first to congratulate you on your purchase of this fine product. This is an actual functioning bank. It can be filled with coins and even money of the paper variety. Once your money is saved, invest it wisely, and send the contents to The Brain c/o ACME LABS, Burbank, CA 91505. May I thank you in advance for your contribution to my efforts in taking over the world." On another side, "Attention: No animal (especially mice) testing was involved in the manufacturing of this fine product.

    Purchase as much Pinky and The Brain merchandise as humanly and financially possible. Persuade your friends and family to do the same.

    Any remaining funds may be sent to The Brain c/o Acme Labs Burbank, CA 91505." $35.00 – 45.00

        Pinky and The Brain cookie jar, 12½" high, "™ & © 96 WB, MADE IN CHINA." On back, "HANDLE CAREFULLY RADIOACTIVE CONTENTS." $65.00 – 75.00

        The Brain and Pinky salt and pepper set, 4" and 6" tall, marked "™ & © '96 WB, MADE IN CHINA." Pinky to Brain: "Hey Brain, can I be the pepper tonight?" Brain to Pinky: "Shut up Pinky or I'll have to 'assault' you!" Pinky to all of us: "Hello. May I be the first to congratulate you on your purchase of this fine product. The perfect addition to any human dwelling. But don't stop here! Be sure to peruse the entire collection of Pinky and The Brain merchandise. All proceeds from the sale of these products will go to a fund which will assist me to take over the world."   Set $28.00 – 32.00

Below: *Dot* figurine, "MADE IN THAILAND TM & © WM 94." $25.00 – 28.00

        Yakko figurine, "MADE IN THAILAND TM & © WB 94." $25.00 – 28.00

        Wakko figurine, "MADE IN THAILAND TM & ©WB 94." $25.00 – 28.00

Row 1:   *Animaniacs* cookie jar, "TM & © 94 WB MADE IN CHINA." $90.00 – 110.00

Row 2:   *Animaniacs* bookends, "TM & ©'95 WB." Paper label "Made in
China." $35.00 – 45.00

Row 3:   *Wakko* bank, "TM & ©'95 WB MADE IN CHINA." $35.00 – 45.00

Animaniacs teapot, "DESIGNED EXCLUSIVELY FOR THE WARNER BROS.
STUDIO STORE TM & © WARNER BROS. WB 1994 MADE IN CHINA." $25.00 – 35.00

Below: *Animaniacs Tower* bank, "MADE IN CHINA TM & © 94 WB." $30.00 – 35.00

Row 1: *New York Giants Taz,* "Team NFL TM/© 1994 NFLP TM & © 1994
WARNER BROS. INC. CERTIFIED INTERNATIONAL CORP. CHINA." $45.00 – 55.00

New York Jets Taz, "Team NFL TM/© 1994 NFLP TM & © 1994 WARNER
BROS. INC. CERTIFIED INTERNATIONAL CORP. CHINA." $45.00 – 55.00

Buffalo Bills Taz, "Team NFL TM/© 1994 NFLP TM & © 1994 WARNER
BROS. INC. CERTIFIED INTERNATIONAL CORP. CHINA." $45.00 – 55.00

Row 2: *Kansas City Chiefs Taz,* "Team NFL TM/© 1994 NFLP TM & © 1994
WARNER BROS. INC. CERTIFIED INTERNATIONAL CORP. CHINA." $45.00 – 55.00

Arizona Cardinals Taz, "Team NFL TM/© 1994 NFLP TM & © 1994
WARNER BROS. INC. CERTIFIED INTERNATIONAL CORP. CHINA." $45.00 – 55.00

San Francisco 49ers Taz, "Team NFL TM/© 1994 NFLP TM & © 1994
WARNER BROS. INC. CERTIFIED INTERNATIONAL CORP. CHINA." $45.00 – 55.00

Row 3: *Pittsburgh Steelers Taz,* "Team NFL TM/© 1994 NFLP TM & © 1994
WARNER BROS. INC. CERTIFIED INTERNATIONAL CORP. CHINA." $45.00 – 55.00

Miami Dolphins Taz, "Team NFL TM/© 1994 NFLP TM & © 1994
WARNER BROS. INC. CERTIFIED INTERNATIONAL CORP. CHINA." $45.00 – 55.00

New England Patriots Taz, "Team NFL TM/© 1994 NFLP TM & © 1994
WARNER BROS. INC. CERTIFIED INTERNATIONAL CORP. CHINA." $45.00 – 55.00

Below: *Chicago Bears Taz,* "Team NFL TM/© 1994 NFLP TM & © 1994
WARNER BROS. INC. CERTIFIED INTERNATIONAL CORP. CHINA." $45.00 – 55.00

Dallas Cowboys Taz, "Team NFL TM/© 1994 NFLP TM & © 1994
WARNER BROS. INC. CERTIFIED INTERNATIONAL CORP. CHINA." $45.00 – 55.00

Green Bay Packers Taz, "Team NFL TM/© 1994 NFLP TM & © 1994
WARNER BROS. INC. CERTIFIED INTERNATIONAL CORP. CHINA." $45.00 – 55.00

Oakland Raiders Taz, "Team NFL TM/© 1994 NFLP TM & © 1994
WARNER BROS. INC. CERTIFIED INTERNATIONAL CORP. CHINA." $45.00 – 55.00

Row 1: *Foghorn-Leghorn with Dog and Henry Hawk,* "TM & © WB 1996 MADE IN CHINA." $65.00 – 75.00

Foghorn-Leghorn utensil holder, "TM & ©1995 WB MADE IN CHINA." $20.00 – 25.00

Foghorn-Leghorn, "TM & © 1993 Warner Bros. Inc. CERTIFIED INTERNATIONAL CORP. TAIWAN." Part of the series of 12 Warner Brothers character jars produced by Certified International. $50.00 – 60.00

Row 2: *Baseball Bugs,* "TM & © 1993 Warner Bros. Inc. CERTIFIED INTERNATIONAL CORP. TAIWAN." Part of the series of 12 Warner Brothers character jars produced by Certified International. $35.00 – 45.00

Bugs with Carrot, "TM & ©1993 Warner Bros. Inc. CERTIFIED INTERNATIONAL CORP. TAIWAN." Part of the series of 12 Warner Brothers character jars produced by Certified International. $35.00 – 45.00

Daffy Baseball, "TM & ©1993 Warner Bros. Inc. CERTIFIED INTERNATIONAL CORP. TAIWAN." Part of the series of 12 Warner Brothers character jars produced by Certified International. $35.00 – 45.00

Row 3: *Roadrunner and Wile E. Coyote,* "TM & ©1993 Warner Bros. Inc. CERTIFIED INTERNATIONAL CORP. TAIWAN." Part of the series of 12 Warner Brothers character jars produced by Certified International. $35.00 – 45.00

Roadrunner, the hard-to-find twelfth jar in a series of 12 Warner Bros. characters produced by Certified International Corp., "TM & ©1993 Warner Bros. Inc. CERTIFIED INTERNATIONAL CORP. TAIWAN." $600.00 – 650.00

Wile E. Coyote, "TM & ©1993 Warner Bros. Inc. CERTIFIED INTERNATIONAL CORP. TAIWAN." Part of the series of 12 Warner Brothers character jars produced by Certified International. $35.00 – 45.00

Below: *Wile E. Coyote* on rocket bank. Grogan. $225.00 – 250.00

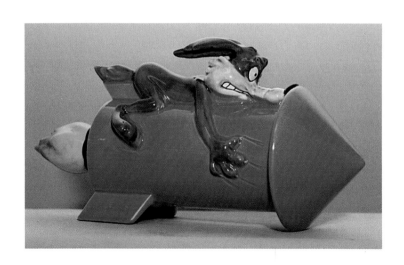

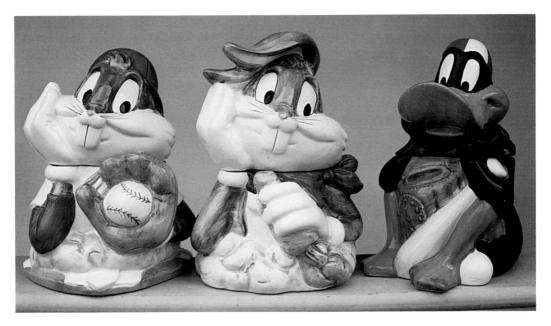

Row 1:   *Bugs Bunny Head,* "MADE IN CHINA TM & © '96 WB" incised into
bottom of jar. $65.00 – 75.00

Bugs Bunny Head, tall ears, "TM & ©1994 Warner Bros. INC. MADE
IN TAIWAN" on transparent label that could easily be removed.
Six Flags exclusive.   Issue price $34.99

Row 2:   *Bugs in the Hole* (front and back), "TM & © '96 W B MADE IN CHINA." Issue price $40.00

Wile E. Coyote and Roadrunner, "TM & © '96 WB MADE IN CHINA." $35.00 – 45.00

Row 3:   *Bugs Miranda,* "TM & © 1994 Warner Bros. MADE IN CHINA." Produced
by Certified International for Warner Brothers. $90.00 – 110.00

Gossamer and Bugs Bunny (front and back), 11½" high, "TM & © 96 WB MADE
IN CHINA" incised into bottom of base. Gossamer first appeared in the
Chuck Jones animated feature, "Hair Raising Hare" in 1946. This is the
only time he has ever appeared in a Warner Brothers production. He
has however, developed quite a significant following and has become
quite popular.
  His most outstanding feature, besides being big, orange, and furry,
would be his tennis shoes. He appeared first as a mean monster,
but his sweet side showed its face once Bugs gave him a makeover
and did his nails. Gossamer is truly a big sweety at heart! *Cookie
Jarrin'* July/August 1996. $75.00 – 85.00

Liberty Bugs, "TM & © 1996 WB MADE IN CHINA." Exclusive to catalog
and New York store.   Issue price $40.00

Below: *Garden Shop,* "TM & © 1997 WARNER BROS MADE IN CHINA" incised
into bottom of base. $45.00 – 50.00

Marc Anthony and Pussyfoot cookie jar, 9" x 10", "TM & © 95
WB MADE IN CHINA." $65.00 – 75.00

Row 1: *Space Jam* bank, "DESIGNED EXCLUSIVELY FOR THE WARNER BROS. STUDIO STORE MADE IN CHINA TM & © WARNER BROS. 1996" on stopper. $40.00 – 50.00

Michael Jordan/Bugs Bunny Space Jam cookie jar, 11"h x 10"w, "TM & © 1996 WB MADE IN CHINA." $80.00 – 100.00

Row 2: *Speedy Gonzales* cookie jar, 11" x 7", "TM & © 96 WB MADE IN CHINA."   Issue price $40.00

Yosemite Sam cookie jar, "TM & © 1993 Warner Bros. Inc. CERTIFIED INTERNATIONAL CORP. TAIWAN." $40.00 – 50.00

Row 3: *WB Characters* bank (front and back), "TM & © '95 WB MADE IN CHINA." $50.00 – 65.00

Below: *London Tour Bus* bank, "DESIGNED EXCLUSIVELY FOR THE WARNER BROS. STUDIO STORE TM & © 1995 WARNER BROS. MADE IN CHINA." $60.00 – 75.00

Bugs Bunny telephone, "TOSHIBA corded telephone model no lt800bug. complies with part 68 fcc rules fcc registration no. AJXCHN-30479-TF-E ringer equivalence no. 1.0B use jack type USOC RJ11C. serial no 610A001921 Toshiba America Consumer Products, Inc. MADE IN CHINA." In addition, "This device complies with part 15 of the FCC rules operation is subject to the following two conditions (1) this device may not cause harmful interference, and (2) this device must accept any interference received, including interference that may cause undesired operation. CAUTION: always disconnect all telephone lines from the wall outlets before servicing or disassembling this equipment, read operating manual before using." $60.00 – 75.00

Bugs Bunny telephone, TM & © WARNER BROS. INC. 1982." Bottom of base, "COM VU I." $100.00 – 125.00

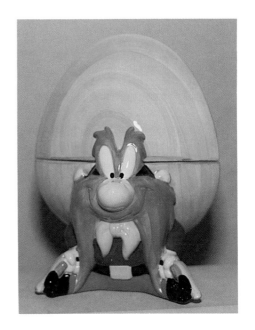

Row 1: *Sylvester* canister, part of 4-piece set, incised "TM & ©95," stamped
"MADE IN CHINA." $65.00 – 75.00

Bugs canister, part of 4-piece set, incised "TM & ©95." stamped
"MADE IN CHINA." $55.00 – 65.00

Taz canister, part of 4-piece set, incised "TM & ©95," stamped
"MADE IN CHINA." $55.00 – 65.00

Tweety canister, part of 4-piece set, incised "TM & ©95," stamped
"MADE IN CHINA." $65.00 – 75.00

Row 2: *Christmas Bugs* salt or pepper shaker, Certified International
prototype, never put in production.   Value not determined.

Christmas Taz salt or pepper shaker, Certified International
prototype, never put in production.   Value not determined.

Christmas Taz, one of six (?) samples by Certified International
Corp., 10" high, unmarked except for paper label, "Item No.
623340" and TRANS-WORLD/TAIWAN."   Value not determined.

Christmas Bugs shaker, Certified International Corp., "TM &
©93 Warner Bros." Hamburg.   Set $18.00 – 22.00

Christmas Taz shaker, Certified International Corp., "TM & ©93
Warner Bros." Hamburg.   Set $18.00 – 22.00

Row 3: *Taz Raiders* cylinder, Certified International, "TO: CIC ITEMS
NO. 623307 Raiders TRANS-WORLD/TAIWAN." Sample $100.00+

Taz and Mrs. Taz salt and pepper set, "TM & © 96 WB MADE IN CHINA"
on each. $32.00 – 38.00

Tasmanian Devil Head, "TM & © 96 WB MADE IN CHINA." $55.00 – 65.00

Right: *WB Characters* Christmas cylinder,
Certified International prototype,
never put in production.
                           Value not determined.

Row 1: *Tweety,* sitting w/cookies, part of the series of 12 Warner
Bros. character jars produced by Cert. Int'l., "TM & © 1993 Warner
Bros. Inc. CERTIFIED INTERNATIONAL CORP. TAIWAN." $35.00 – 45.00

Sylvester holding Tweety's cage, talking, "TM & © 1993 Warner
Bros. Inc. CERTIFIED INTERNATIONAL CORP. TAIWAN." Part of the
series of 12 Warner Bros. character jars produced by Cert. Intl. $50.00 – 60.00

Row 2: *Tweety* and *Christmas Tree* salt shaker, "TM & © 95 WB, MADE IN
CHINA."   Set $18.00 – 22.00

Tweety Christmas Ornament cookie jar, 10"h x 8"w, impressed into
bottom of the base, "TM & © 96 WB, MADE IN CHINA." Removable
decal "DESIGNED EXCLUSIVELY FOR THE WARNER BROS. STUDIO STORE
TM & © WARNER BROS. 1996, MADE IN CHINA. $65.00 – 75.00

Sylvester and Christmas Tree pepper shaker, "TM & © 95 WB, MADE IN
CHINA."   Set $18.00 – 22.00

Row 3: *Tweety Christmas Stocking,* "TM © 1993 Warner Bros. Inc. CERTIFIED
INTERNATIONAL CORP. CHINA." $100.00 – 125.00

Tweety Ornament salt shaker, "TM & © 95 WB MADE IN CHINA."   Set $23.00 – 28.00

Taz Santa, "TM © 95 WB MADE IN CHINA." $70.00 – 80.00

Sylvester Ornament pepper shaker, "TM & © 95 WB, MADE IN
CHINA."   Set $23.00 – 28.00

Bugs Santa, "TM © 1993 Warner Bros. Inc. CERTIFIED INTERNATIONAL
CORP. CHINA." $90.00 – 110.00

Below: *Bugs Bunny in Carrot Bag,* "©WARNER BROS. INC. 1981," distributed
by Gorham. Bady. $325.00 – 375.00

Bugs Magician, Certified International Corp. sample.   Value not determined.

Row 1: *Summer Olympics,* Atlanta, GA 1996, "TM & © 96 WB MADE IN CHINA." $100.00 – 125.00

Row 2: *Summer Olympics,* Atlanta, GA 1996, "TM & © 96 WB MADE IN CHINA." $100.00 – 125.00

Below: *Daffy Duck,* ceramic with polyresin finial (Daffy and top lid). Issued in celebration of Daffy Duck's 60th Birthday, April 17, 1997. Impressed into bottom of base "™ & © 97 WB MADE IN CHINA." Issue price $40.00

Daffy Duck Head, "TM & © 1994 Warner Bros. INC. MADE IN TAIWAN" on removable, transparent, label. Six Flags Theme Park exclusive. Issue price $34.99

Bugs Bunny glass cylinder (Anchor Hocking), "TM & ©1994 Warner Bros." $15.00 – 18.00

Bugs Bunny cylinder, "TM & ©1993 WARNER BROS. INC. CERTIFIED INTERNATIONAL CORP. TAIWAN." $18.00 – 22.00

Row 1: *Sylvester* teakettle, stamped on circular black label with white lettering "M. KAMENSTEIN INC. TAIWAN • © MCMXCIV, KAMENSTEIN ® U.S. AND FOREIGN PATENTS PENDING." On outer edge of label, "TM & © 1994 WARNER BROS." $25.00 – 35.00

Tweety Head cookie jar, smaller size, "TM & © 1995 SIX FLAGS THEME PARKS INC. TM & © 1995." Paper label "MADE IN TAIWAN." Issue price $31.99

Row 2: *Tweety Head* cookie jar, 11⅝" high, "TM & © 96 WB MADE IN CHINA." $65.00 – 75.00

Sylvester Head (with Tweety) cookie jar, "APPLAUSE INC. WOODLAND HILLS, CA 91365 TM & © 1994 WARNER BROTHERS LOONEY TUNES CHARACTERS, NAMES AND ALL RELATED INDICIA ARE TRADEMARKS OF WARNER © 1993. MADE IN TAIWAN 29185 SYLVESTER™/ TWEETY™ NOT DISHWASHER SAFE HAND WASH ONLY." $70.00 – 80.00

Row 3: *Sylvester,* sitting, largest canister in 4-piece set, "TM & © 95 WB MADE IN CHINA." $65.00 – 75.00

Sylvester Peering Over Tweety's Cage, "TM & © 95 WB MADE IN CHINA." $65.00 – 75.00

Below: *Sylvester on Treasure Chest* bank, © Warner Bros. Inc. 1981. Silver-colored label "FROM THE GIFT WORLD OF GORHAM MADE IN JAPAN." $25.00 – 35.00

Tweety bank, "TM & © Warner Bros., Made Exclusively for the Warner Bros. Studio Store." Incised TM & © 1995 WARNER BROS. MADE IN CHINA." Issue price $20.00

Grandma and Sylvester salt and pepper set. Grandma, "TM & © '95 WB MADE IN CHINA." Sylvester, "TM & © '95 WB." $32.00 – 38.00

Sylvester clock, "TM & © 95 WB." Issue price $30.00

Row 1:   *Porky Pig* ceramic bank, 9" high, "TM & © '94 WB MADE IN CHINA."   Issue price $18.00

Porky Pig (in TV) cookie jar, 10½" x 8½", "TM & © '95 WB MADE IN CHINA." $55.00 – 65.00

Row 2:   *Scooby and Snacks* stackable salt and pepper set. "TM & © 1997 HANNA-BARBERA MADE IN CHINA." Paper label, DESIGNED EXCLUSIVELY FOR THE WARNER BROS. STUDIO STORE MADE IN CHINA TM & © WARNER BROS. 1997." $18.00 – 22.00

Scooby-Doo cookie jar, incised "©HANNA-BARBERA CARTOONS, INC. HANNA-BARBERA PRODUCTIONS, INC. MADE IN CHINA." Paper label, "DESIGNED EXCLUSIVELY FOR THE WARNER BROS. STUDIO STORE MADE IN CHINA. TM & © WARNER BROS. 1997.   Reissued $40.00

Row 3:   *Caffe Pepe* (Pepe Le Pew) cookie jar, 12" x 10", "Designed Exclusively for the Warner Bros. Studio Store TM & © 1995 Warner Bros. Made in China." $55.00 – 65.00

Pepe and Penelope salt and pepper set, "TM & © 1994 Warner Bros. INC. MADE IN CHINA." $32.00 – 38.00

Pepe and Penelope cookie jar, 12" x 11½", "TM & © 96 WB MADE IN CHINA." $90.00 – 110.00

Below: *Sylvester on Cookie Can,* "TM & © 1994 Warner Bros. INC. MADE IN TAIWAN." $70.00 – 80.00

Taz in Cookie Jar, "Applause Inc. Woodland Hills, CA 91365 TM & © 1994 WARNER BROS. LOONEY TUNES, characters, names, and all related indicia are trademarks of Warner Bros. © 1993. MADE IN TAIWAN 29186 TASMANIAN DEVIL™ NOT DISHWASHER SAFE HAND WASH ONLY CE." $65.00 – 75.00

Row 1: *Marvin in Spaceship* stacking salt and pepper set, "© '93 Warner Bros. C.I.C. CHINA." — $18.00 – 22.00

Marvin in Spaceship cookie jar, "TM & © 1993 Warner Bros. Inc. CERTIFIED INTERNATIONAL CORP. TAIWAN." — $60.00 – 70.00

Marvin the Martian letter organizer, "TM & © 95 WB." Paper label "MADE IN CHINA." — Issue price $16.00

Row 2: *Marvin the Martian Head* cookie jar, stamped on dry pottery rim, bottom of base "TM & © 1995 SIX FLAGS THEME PARKS INC., TM & © 1995 WARNER BROS." Small rectangular foil label "MADE IN TAIWAN." — Issue price $34.99

Marvin and K-9 salt and pepper set, "TM & © 95 WB MADE IN CHINA." — $28.00 – 32.00

K-9 (Marvin the Martian's dog), "ACME PET SHOP SUPPLY COMPANY TM & © 1996 WARNER BROS. MADE IN CHINA." — $85.00 – 95.00

Row 3: *Marvin the Martian* alarm clock, "LOONEY TUNES, characters, names and all related indicia are trademarks of Warner Bros. © 1993 MADE IN CHINA." — $15.00 – 18.00

Marvin the Martian soakie, "TM 1995 MADE IN CHINA." Paper label "TM & ©1996 WARNER BROS." — $8.00 – 10.00

Marvin in Spaceship bank, composition, "TM & ©94 WB." Paper label "Made in China." — $24.00 – 26.00

Below: *Marvin with Ray Gun,* "TM & © 95 WB MADE IN CHINA." — $80.00 – 90.00

WATT POTTERY

Watt Pottery was established in Crooksville, Ohio, in 1922, though it wasn't until 1936 kitchen utility ware, including cookie jars, started. In 1965, the factory was destroyed by fire, never to be reopened. Normally when collectors think of Watt Apple, they envision cylinders with hand-painted apples. What a fantastic find.

Below: *Apple* cookie jar with original packing box. Howard.   Price not determined.

THE NATIONAL COOKIE JAR SHOW

Walter F. Sill, Jr., established The National Cookie Jar Show as part of the Nashville Antique Festival in 1994. This show is held the first weekend in May, at the Tennessee State Fairgrounds in Nashville, Tennessee.

Row 1: *1995 Squiggy Squirrel.* $35.00 – 45.00

1996 Nashville Truck, "JC Miller" incised into pottery. Written underglaze, "3rd Annual National Cookie Jar Show 1996, ____/100." Written on card included with jar: "Nashville Truck, This jar depicts a cookie jar dealer on the way to Nashville, Tenn. He has a full load of wonderful cookie jars to sell or trade. Model by Jerry P Miller." Issue price $125.00

Row 2: *1997 Leprechaun,* "SCULPTED BY DON WINTON, OFFICIAL JAR 1997 4TH ANNUAL COOKIE JAR SHOW, LIMITED EDITION OF 200." Issue price $150.00

1998 Puss 'n Boots, "COMMEMORATIVE COOKIE JAR PRODUCED BY THE NEW ROSE COLLECTION 19©90, SCULPTED BY DON WINTON." Issue price $89.95

REPRODUCTIONS

In the Beginning

Reproductions have had the single-most detrimental effect on the cookie jar market since the publication of *The Collector's Encyclopedia of Cookie Jars* in 1991. They seemed innocent enough at first. They would provide an attractive, inexpensive alternative for collectors who couldn't afford the originals, and would be an additional source of income for dealers. But collectors and dealers alike were unanimous; they must be properly identified so no one would be hurt. Everyone assumed manufacturers would conform, producing a clearly-marked product. Not so. While many manufacturers were responsible, some sold unmarked jars fully realizing that these jars could (and in too many instances would) be sold as originals.

Additionally, no thought was given to the fact that reproducing character jars was not only immoral but illegal. It infringes on; both copyright laws and licensing agreements. Be alert to unlicensed products being sold as legitimate, licensed pieces.

As time went on, it dawned upon us; these reproductions were not cheap. Granted they were less expensive than the original, but people were paying substantial sums for what, a shelf piece? Not to mention the fact that every time someone chose to buy these "pacifiers" instead of the original, the value of the original depreciated.

Manufacturers of Reproductions

There seem to be four major manufacturers of reproductions. One is located in West Allis, Wisconsin; two in the Zanesville, Ohio, area; and the New McCoy Pottery, billing itself as manufacturing "antique reproductions," in Spring City, Tennessee.

The McCoy name is probably one of the most recognized names in the pottery industry; everyone automatically assumes a marked piece to be "The Real McCoy." Here's the history of The New McCoy Pottery. The owner of this pottery seized the opportunity to capitalize on the McCoy name. He had his lawyers file a trademark for the McCoy name and began putting it on the bottom of his jars. This registration was challenged by Ralph Porto, owner of Designer Accents, who bought McCoy from the Lancaster Colony Group in 1985. Despite erroneous information to the contrary, Porto registered McCoy as a trademark on June 25, 1991. (Interestingly enough, Jensen's trademark, filed on August 31, 1992, reads exactly as Porto's.) Though Designer Accents closed for the 1990 holiday season and has not reopened to date, Porto still owns the McCoy name. The New McCoy Pottery ceased using the McCoy trademark, instead marking their ware "Brush-McCoy." (Brush McCoy never made cookie jars!) This too was challenged. Effective October 1997, Jensen is no longer legally able to use McCoy in any form on his product. As of this writing, their wares (when marked) are identified as "B.M. Hull." Buyer, beware!

Some Examples

Chiquita Prestwood of North Carolina, a veteran McCoy collector, warned of fake McCoy green Gleeps in the July 1997 *NMXpress.* She was tempted to buy one during the 1996 Zanesville, Ohio, Pottery Festival. It was heavy and appeared genuine. Fortunately, she was able to compare the questionable jar to a real one on display at the Ohio Ceramics Center in Crooksville. Upon comparison, differences were obvious. The original was taller and larger overall; the paint was evenly applied and rich in color. The colorization of the fake was uneven and lighter in several areas; the method of airbrushing was different. Somehow, stories have circulated that the real green Gleeps were test pieces and would be smaller. That's not correct. They are 10½", the same size as the more common yellow Gleeps.

A perfect Watt Policeman cookie jar sold at auction in Maine (March 1996) for $1,325.00. The winning bidder claimed to be an agent for an absentee buyer who was going to use the jar as a model for reproductions. These have appeared on the market. The unmarked original is 10¼" to 10½" high; the forgery is 9¾" high.

Early in 1997 several pieces of Little Red Riding Hood were sold through auction on the Internet. They included a 12½" high cookie jar marked "967 Hull, Little Red Riding Hood, Pat. Applied For USA," an 8¾" wall pocket, a 6" standing milk pitcher (sold as an open creamer), and a 4½" pair of shakers (sold as rare 4" medium shakers), the last four pieces unmarked.

We wish we had a nickel for all the calls we've gotten concerning the Little Red Riding Hood jar marked "McCoy" (from the New McCoy Pottery). It doesn't matter if your jar appears old; crackle glaze was deliberately used to make them look that way. Remember, the original McCoy Pottery *never* made a Red Riding Hood jar, or anything else associated with Red Riding Hood.

A Buckeye Lake, Ohio, ceramist produced a Smokey Bear head without benefit of license. Even after being served with a cease and desist order by the Department of Agriculture, the bear continued to be sold, but with a hat embossed with "Cookey." A second hat that said "Smokey" was given to the customers as a bonus. So much for integrity.

Where We Are Now

Many a slick sales job has been given the unsuspecting, novice collector. A tidy profit lines the salesman's palm and you own a reproduction that will never magically turn into an original (or, for that matter, accrue in value). The choice is yours. Ask yourself: "Would I be better off investing my money into an attractive jar that has not been reproduced?" We feel that many of the jars on the market today will become collectible in varying degrees, especially those of limited production.

Known Reproductions

As an aid to collectors and dealers, we have compiled the following list of known reproductions. There may be others, and there are new ones all the time. These, as well as unlicensed items, are covered in the *Cookie Jarrin'* newsletter.

Reproductions

Abingdon

Choo Choo
Hobby Horse
Humpty Dumpty
Little Bo Peep
Little Old Lady
Miss Muffet
Mother Goose

American Bisque

Baby Huey
Casper salt & pepper set
Chalkboard
  Boy
  Clown
  Girl
  Hobo
  Saddle
Dino (Flinstones)
Elephant w/ball cap
Fred Flinstone
Fred/Wilma Bank
Happy Clown
Horse
Little Lulu
Mohawk Indian
Olive Oyl
Pig w/straw hat
Popeye
Popeye bank
Rubbles House (Flintstones)
Saddle w/o chalkboard
Truck
Wilma on Telephone

Artistic Pottery

Chef
Mammy
Mammy salt & pepper

Brayton Laguna

Maid
Mammy
Matilda

Brush

Chick and Nest
Circus Horse
Covered Wagon
Cow w/cat finial, brown,
  black/white,
  purple/white, and
  blue /white
Davy Crockett
Donkey and Cart
Elephant (wearing baby hat)
Fish
Formal Pig, black, yellow,
  and green coat,
  w & w/o gold trim
Granny
Hillbilly Frog
Humpty Dumpty in Beanie
Laughing Hippo
Little Boy Blue
Little Red Riding Hood
Peter Pan
Little Angel
Little Girl
Old Shoe
Panda

Puppy Police
Sitting Pig
Smiling Bear

California Originals

Cookie Monster
Ernie
Oscar the Grouch
Superman, brown & silver
The Count
Wonder Woman

Cleminson

King

DeForest

Halo Boy
Parrot

Enesco

Chef
Mammy

Gilner

Mammy
Mammy shaker

Gonder

Pirate
Sheriff

Hull

Little Red Riding Hood
  cookie jar
  cream & sugar
  salt & pepper shakers
  teapot
  wall pocket

Japan

Basket-handle Butler
  biscuit jar
  cookie jar
Basket-handle Mammy
  biscuit jar
  butter dish
  cookie jar
  cream & sugar
  match safe
  napkin holder
  salt & pepper set
  sprinkle bottle
  string holder
  toothpick holder
Blond-haired Mammy
Googly-eyed Mammy
  biscuit jar
  cookie jar
Mammy
Chef

Lane

Indian
Sheriff

Lefton

Winking Santa

Ludowici Celadon

Bear Turnabout

McCoy

Cauliflower Mammy
Chairman of the Board
Clown Bust
Dalmatians (in Rocking Chair)
Davy Crockett
Gleep, green & yellow
Hobby Horse
Indian
  Leprechaun, red, green,
  & multicolor
Mammy, white & decorated
  green (aqua blue) yellow
Tepee

Metlox

Calf Head
Chef Pierre
Mammy
Pinocchio
Puddles
Raccoon Bandit
Scrub Woman
Teddy Bear

Miscellaneous

Cinderella
Luzianne Mammy
  salt & pepper set
Polka Dot Mammy
Gold-teeth Mammy
Cream of Wheat Chef
  salt & pepper shakers
Sears Little Girl in pink
  & blue (never made for
  Sears in blue)

Mosaic Tile

Mammy

National Silver

Chef
Mammy salt & pepper

Pearl China

Chef and Mammy
  salt & pepper sets

Pottery Guild

Elsie

Red Wing

Katrina (Dutch Girl)
Pierre (Chef)

Regal

Goldilocks
Peek-a-Boo
  salt & pepper shakers

Royal Ware

Bear

Robinson-Ransbottom

Cow Over Moon

Shawnee

Corn
Lucky elephant
Muggsy
Puss 'n Boots
Sailor (GOB)
Smiley regular & bank head
Winnie regular & bank head

Sierra Vista

Davy Crockett

Sigma

Kliban Mama Cat

Treasure Craft

Nanna

Twin Winton

Ark
Barn canister set
Dutch Girl
Elf Stump
Flopsy (Raggedy Andy)
Hillbilly bank
Mopsy (Raggedy Ann)
Mother Goose
Sailor Elephant
Scioto Santa

Vallona Starr

Winky

Vandor

Popeye Head

Walt Disney

Big Al
Dumbo Turnabout
  (never distributed by
  Leeds in gray under-
  glaze color)
Mickey/Minnie
  Turnabout
Roly Dalmatian

Weller

Watermelon Mammy
  batter bowl
  cookie jar
  creamer/sugar
  syrup pitcher
  teapot

Watt

Policeman

Reproduction Red Riding Hood
This was purchased off the Internet.

Original McCoy Davy Crockett on left.

Original Lane Sheriff on left.

Original Brush Cow on right.

Left to right: Mexico, China, McCoy.

Original plaid apron Mammy on right

Original Watt policeman on right.

Mark on Smiley Pig reproduction.

Reproductions marked McCoy, Brush McCoy, or BM Hull.

Mark on Cow Over Moon reproduction.

Original ABC Swee' Pea on left.

Original ABC Popeye on left.

Note enlongated base and loss of detail on the left cookie jar.

The Original McCoy Cauliflower Mammy is on the right.

Original Brush Peter
Pan on right.

Original Brush Angel
on right.

Original ABC Rubbles'
House on right.

BIBLIOGRAPHY

Carey, Larry and Sylvia Tompkins. *1003 Salt & Pepper Shakers with Values.* Atglen, Pennsylvania: Schiffer Publishing Ltd., 1997.

DeLozier, Loretta. *Collector's Encyclopedia of Lefton China, Identification & Values.* Paducah, Kentucky: Collector Books, 1995.

___. *Collector's Encyclopedia of Lefton China Book II, Identification & Values.* Paducah, Kentucky: Collector Books, 1997.

Gibbs, Carl, Jr. *Collector's Encyclopedia of Metlox Potteries, Identification and Values.* Paducah, Kentucky: Collector Books, 1995.

Roerig, Fred and Joyce Herndon Roerig, *The Collector's Encyclopedia of Cookie Jars.* Paducah, Kentucky: Collector Books, 1991.

___. *Collector's Encyclopedia of Cookie Jars, Book II.* Paducah, Kentucky: Collector Books, 1991.

Roerig, Joyce Herndon, *Cookie Jarrin', The Cookie Jar Newsletter.* Volumes 1–7. Charter year 1991. RR2 Box 504, Walterboro, South Carolina 29488.

Warner & Posgay. *The World of Wade, Book 2, Collectable Porcelain and Pottery.* Marietta, Ohio: Antique Publications, 1994.

ADDITIONAL SOURCES

Curran, Pamela Duvall. *Shawnee Pottery, The Full Encyclopedia.* Atglen, Pennsylvania: Schiffer Publishing, Ltd., 1995.

Duke, Harvey. *The Official Price Guide to Pottery and Porcelain.* New York: House of Collectibles, 1995.

Sanford, Martha and Steve. *The Guide to Brush-McCoy Pottery.* Self published: Martha and Steve Sanford, 230 Harrison Avenue, Campbell, California 95008. 1992.

Schneider, Mike. *The Complete Cookie Jar Book.* Atglen, Pennsylvania: Schiffer Publishing, Ltd., 1991.

Westfall, Ermagene. *An Illustrated Value Guide to Cookie Jars.* Paducah, Kentucky: Collector Books, 1993.

___. *An Illustrated Value Guide to Cookie Jars, Book II.* Paducah, Kentucky: Collector Books, 1993.

CLUBS AND NEWSLETTERS

Abel, Dominick and Kathleen Moloney, *Shawnee News,* 211 West 92nd Street, Box #42, New York, New York 10025, Fax: 212-595-3133, E-mail: kmda@aol.com.

Clark, Lanette, Haeger Pottery Collectors of America, 5021 Toyon Way, Antioch, CA 94509.

DeLozier, Loretta. *The Lefton Collector,* 1101, Polk St., Bedford, Iowa 50833. E-mail: LeftonLady@aol.com.

Roerig, Joyce Herndon. *Cookie Jarrin', The Cookie Jar Newsletter,* Route 2, Box 504, Walterboro, South Carolina 29488. $29.95 per year.

International Association of Jim Beam Bottle and Specialities Clubs, 2015 Burlington Ave., Kewanee, Illinois 61443.

Seman, Carol. *The NM Express* (a monthly McCoy bulletin), 7670 Chippewa, Suite 406, Brecksville, Ohio 44141. $26.00 per year. E-mail: McCjs@aol.com.

Thornburg, Irene. Novelty Salt and Pepper Shakers Club, 581 Joy Road, Battle Creek, Michigan 49017. Newsletter included in membership.

Van Meter, Jim. *The Hot Foot Teddy* (Smokey Bear) *Collector Association,* PO Box 1416, Westwood, California 96137. $20.00 per year.

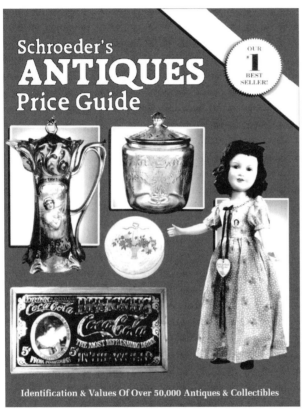